A section of the Plan of London, Westminster and Southwark by John Rocque, 1746.

St James's, London

Calibrachoa 'Union Jack' Preplanted 25cm Hanging Basket

Portrait of Charles II, studio of (?) John Michael Wright, c.1660-5.

ST JAMES'S, LONDON

Joan Glasheen

Phillimore

1987

Published by
PHILLIMORE & CO. LTD.
Shopwyke Hall, Chichester, Sussex

ISBN 0 85033 625 2

Printed and bound in Great Britain by
BIDDLES LTD.,
Guildford, Surrey

This book is dedicated to
Their Royal Highnesses The Duke and Duchess of Kent,
to all my friends and colleagues at York House, past and present,
and to my family, with love

Contents

List of Illustrations

Frontispiece: Portrait of Charles II

Illustration Acknowledgements

The author wishes to thank the following people and institutions for permission to reproduce illustrations in this book: The Library Print Room, Windsor Castle, by gracious permission of Her Majesty the Queen, numbers 5, 32, 93, 103, 108, 116 and 117; BBC/Hulton Picture Library, numbers 9, 11, 12, 15, 16, 17, 18, 20, 21, 23, 24, 25, 26, 27, 39, 47, 75, 77, 90, 94, 95 and 96; British Tourist Authority, numbers 7, 28, 29, 45, and 79; Patric Glasheen, numbers 40, 42, 43, 49, 50, 51, 52, 55, 59, 60, 62, 63, 65, 66 and 68; London Topographical Society, numbers 3 and 4; National Portrait Gallery, numbers 2, 6, 8, 14, 19, 22, 30, 31, 35, 41, 44, 56, 64, 69, 70, 71, 73, 74, 80, 81, 82, 87, 88, 89, 104, 105, 106, 107, 109, 110, 111, 112, 113, 114, 115 and the frontispiece; Westminster Archives Room, Westminster City Council, numbers 1, 3, 4, 10, 33, 34, 38, 45, 53, 54, 57, 58, 61, 67, 72, 76, 78, 84, 85 and 92 (nos. 10, 67, 84 and 85 are from *Georgian London* by Geoffrey Summerson, 1945, and reproduced with permission). Other photographs are from the author's collection.

Acknowledgements

The author wishes to thank the following institutions which have allowed her to do research for this book: The *Cavendish Hotel*, Jermyn Street; The Crown Estate Commissioners; The London Library; The Public Record Office; The Royal Library; and *The Times*. In all these offices work became a pleasure, surrounded by the unfailing courtesy and patience of the staff. May they flourish evermore.

Those who have given permission for the reproduction of illustrations have been acknowledged separately.

Preface

A visitor to London would be keen to see the historic buildings of the ancient city, the museums, the theatres, and to do some shopping. Having seen Westminster Abbey, the Houses of Parliament and Big Ben, Buckingham Palace, and the Tower, he might remember St James's, where the Changing of the Guard begins.

Such a visitor could walk along Piccadilly from the Circus, past Burlington House, Fortnum and Mason, and Hatchard's the Bookshop, and look down St James's Street on the left. At the bottom of the hill he will see a great Gatehouse, with scarlet-coated sentries, guarding an old Tudor palace, where the centuries before 1100 can be traced, through nuns, kings, queens, wars, coronations, mistresses and the plague.

Had he stood in this same spot 900 years ago, he would have seen a pathetic group of wattle and daub buildings in a bare, desolate landscape, the only human habitation near him. Toward the east in the distance, the City of London lies within its Roman walls, the newly-built tower the symbol of the Norman Conqueror. Over sour marshland to the south, on Thorney Island, where the River Tyburn joins the

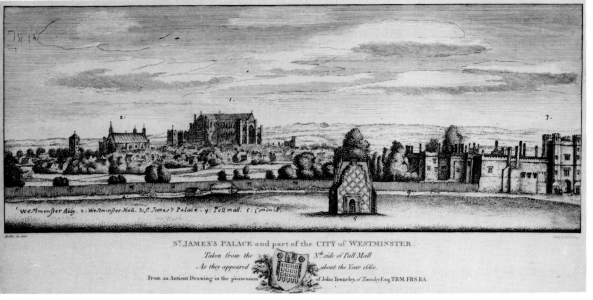

1. St James's Palace from the north side of Pall Mall, 1660. Pell Mell (marked as no. 4) is where Charles II played the game until he moved the site to The Mall, on the other side of St James's Palace.

Thames, lies Westminster Abbey, built by Edward the Confessor, who was buried there in 1065; the scene of William's Coronation in 1066.

In the little valley figures are moving about their work. Who are they? This tiny settlement was St James's Hospital for 'fourteen sisters, maidens that were leprouse, living chastely and honestly in divine service', which was 'laid by well-disposed citizens of London, rigorous against lepers in the City'. It was a lonely, enclosed community, governed by the Abbots of Westminster.

The first lazar houses in the kingdom were St James's and St Giles's in London, well outside the city walls, and Burton St Lazar in the county of Leicestershire. Of these, St James's is by far the oldest. We have no precise date of origin, but a reference is made in the Cotton Manuscripts to a visit by 'Gislebertus' to the hospital, just after the Feast of John the Baptist in 1100.

And in 1987? The site of the lazar house is now a palace, with royal households, the Lord Chamberlain's Office, an incessant swirl of ceremonial processions, guardsmen, tourists, and traffic. For a resident of the palace, as the author has had the great good fortune to be, the questions from tourists are innumerable, the most usual being 'Who lived here?' 'What happened here?' Jolted into research by curiosity, using diarists, historians, letter-writers, biographers, old records and documents, the author discovered a fascinating story spanning 900 years.

If one could look down from the top of the hill in 1100 there would be no Westminster, just a broad and marshy heath where now lie the palaces, Millbank, the great parks and, to the north, dreary swamps, up to the slopes of the hills at Hampstead.

The River Tyburn ran down from the north, round today's Regent's Park, across Oxford Street, Piccadilly and Green Park to Buckingham Palace, where it divided into two branches (one later supplied the lake in St James's Park), which eventually fed into the Thames and encircled an island called Thorney, upon which Westminster Abbey was built.

Why would the hospital have been built here? Partly for isolation of course. But could there have been a practical reason? A gravel bed in that marsh, with a spring of sweet water, a well used by St James's Palace residents, until comparatively recent times? The main building materials would have been round logs or squared beams, with wattle and daub, that is, twigs and supple branches twined together and daubed with mud, with reed-thatched roofs.

After the Norman Conquest in 1066 there was a building boom, but masons and carpenters were still of Anglo-Saxon stock. A new wooden hall would have looked much the same in 1080 as in 1060. Buildings after the Conquest were small and mean, the better houses were timber framed, with shutters and lattices, but no glass for windows. Poorer houses were of wattle and daub. Churches were numerous and small, some were still of wood, a few of stone.

After that architectural opinion, we have some evidence from the 12th century. William Fitzstephen, clerk to Thomas à Becket, Archbishop of Canterbury, wrote a life of his master. In the preface he tells us: 'the walls of the city [were] in good repair ... The Royal Palace [Whitehall] stood outside the city, connected to it by a prosperous suburb [the Strand]'. Those walls, and the Palace, were within sight of the convent-hospital. Over seven hundred years later, during building alterations to the Chapel Royal in 1838, Norman masonry was discovered, so we may, with some reason, assume the leper's tiny chapel was of stone although other buildings were of wood.

Where did they bury their dead? The Capuchin Friars of Queen Henrietta Maria's household in the mid-17th century laid their cemetery just west of the Queen's chapel, according to a map of 1689. Could it have previously been used by the hospital? The answer lies under today's Marlborough Road, between Queen's Chapel and Friary Court.

Some details of the clerks of the hospital in the 13th and 14th centuries survive. In 1286 Brother Godard was the Master; in 1312 Walter de Sutton was the King's Clerk. Other clerks before 1467 included Robert de Dunham, Simon de Bereford, Henry de Purle, Richard Clifford, Thomas Kempe and Roger Malmesbury. In 1379 Thomas de Orgrave was reprimanded for crenellating a small tower, so by then the hospital had definitely acquired stone walls, and the status that went with them.

It is generally supposed that leprosy came to the west as a result of the Crusades, and that the soldiers carried it home with them, but by the early 15th century the disease had ceased to be so prevalent and the hospital became simply a convent. Its chapel was now 300 years old and firmly established as a sacred place. In 1403, for instance, an Irish horse thief called Nicholas Cusak claimed sanctuary here; the horse was priced at 30 shillings.

There had always been disputes between the Abbots of Westminster and the Bishops of London over the administration of the convent, but in 1449 King Henry VI gave the wardenship to Eton College.

In 1532 the first phase of the history of St James's came to an end when King Henry VIII 'compounded with' the sisters, bought the convent, demolished it and built a manor of red bricks. This building was known variously as 'James's House', 'The King's House' and 'The House in the Fields'. It was a hunting lodge, a private refuge for the king, away from the scheming, formal, political court life in the Palace of Westminster, and its construction marked the beginning of the second 450 years of continuous residence in this unique place.

John Stow, an antiquary, and author of the *Survey of London* (1598) (an invaluable source for anyone interested in the history of London), knew St James's shortly after Henry had built his palace.

> Charing Crosse, which cross, builded of stone, was ... there made by commandment of Edward 1st... West from this crosse, stoode sometime an hospital of St James's. This hospital was surrendered to Henry VIII in the third and twentieth year of his reign. The sisters being compounded with were allowed pensions, for Terme of their lives. And the king builded there a goodly Mannor, annexing thereunto a park, closed about with a wall of bricke, now called St James's Park – serving indifferently the said mannor and to the mannor or Pallace of Westminster.

In 1270 King Edward I granted a fair to be kept in James's Field each year, to begin on the eve of St James's Day, (24 July), to last for six days, the profits to go to the hospital, and all shops in the City of London to be closed during that time. One wonders how much this would please the good citizens; remember, 'the city' meant the City of London, centred about St Paul's Cathedral: a long walk, either muddy or dusty. Here is one account of the fair from Mackyn's *Diary of a Resident in London, 1560*, dated 30 July.

2. Portrait of Henry VIII after Hans Holbein, *c.*1536.

4

St James's Fayer by Westminster was so greate that a man could not have a pygg for mony., and the dearrie-wiffes had nother meate nor drinck before 3 o'clock on the same day. And the chese went very well away for a penny of the pounde. Besides the greate and mightee armie of beggars and bandes that ther were.

In 1665 this annual event was moved away from the Palace to St James's Market, which once flourished on the site of what is now Lower Regent Street. Finally, it was sent much further away, to Mayfair, where it continued annually for many years until that area of open country became the fashionable, residential district of the present day.

Before considering St James's Palace itself, it is important to know something of the early development of the streets where all the life of the Palace spilled over – courtiers, ministers, shops, inns, stables and houses. In 1870 Theodore Hook said 'London *par excellence* is bounded on the north by Piccadilly, on the south by Pall Mall, on the east by Haymarket, and on the West by St James's Street' and there is still much truth in this today. Our survey begins with Pall Mall.

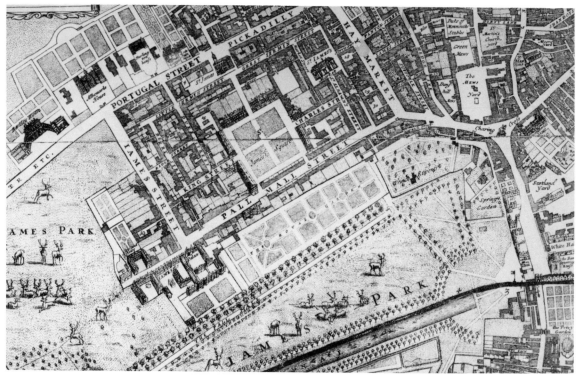

3. Map of the Pall Mall area by Morden and Lee, 1682.

4. Map of the same area by Harwood, 1792.

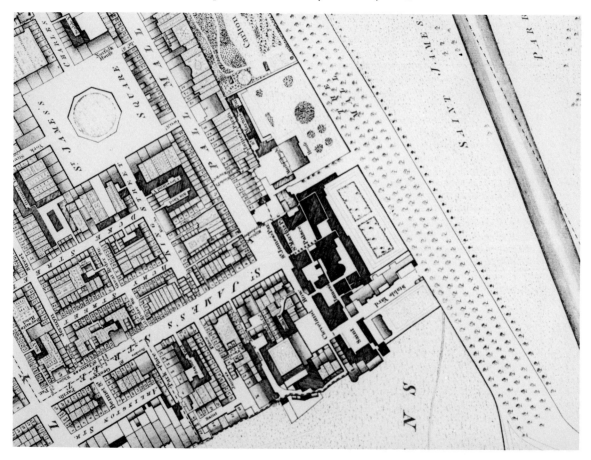

Pall Mall

Before 1066 this was a simple muddy country road, running west from the Whitehall Mews on the site of what is now Trafalgar Square, where the kings kept their falcons, to the Great Gate of St James's Palace, as Faithorne's map of 1608 shows. There were fields on the northern side reaching up to Piccadilly which was also a minor country road. Jesse, in 1847, quotes a writer called Anderson, 'who wrote in the middle of the last century' (1740-60) as saying, 'I have met with several old persons in my younger days who remembered when there was but one house, a cake house, between the Mews gate and St James's Great Gate'.

The Sieur de la Serre, a French visitor to London in 1638, describes what he saw of Pall Mall: 'Near the avenue of the Palace is a large meadow, always green, in which the ladies walk in Summer; Its great gate has a long street in front, leading to the fields. The Palace is built of red brick, very ancient, with a flat, leaden roof and is surrounded by crennels.' That roof is still of lead today. 'In which the Ladies walk' – perhaps they picnicked under the apple trees for which these fields were famous.

Pall Mall formed part of the route taken by the rebel leader, Sir Thomas Wyatt, marching with his men from the west, across Hyde Park Corner and Green Park, past St James's Palace, and on towards the city in his attempt upon London in 1554. He failed, yet he created immense panic both in the City and in court circles. There was a battle at St James's, and I can do no better than quote Stow:

> On February 6th, 1554, about 5 o'clock, a trumpeter went about and warned all horsemen and men-at-arms to be at St James's field, and all footmen to be there by 6 o'clock next morning... The scouts said Wyatt was at Brentford, which made all the court wonderfully afraid. Drums beat through London at 4.00 a.m., commanding all soldiers to armour, and so to Charing Cross. Wyatt, hearing Pembroke was in the field, stayed at Knightsbridge until next day. By ten of the clock, Pembroke had set his horsemen on the hill above St James's. His footmen were set in two battles, somewhat lower and nearer Charing Cross, and his ordnance on the hillside. In the mean season, Wyatt planted his ordnance on a hill beyond St James's, over against the park corner, and after a few words to his men, came down the lane on foot, hard by the Court Gate at St James's Palace. Pembroke's men hovered until all passed but the tail, which they did set upon, and cut off. The others marched on, and never returned to the aid of their tail. They shot off freshly on both sides; A piece of ordnance slew three of Wyatt's men in a rank, and after carrying off their heads, passed through the wall into the park. At Charing Cross, stood Sir John Gage with the Guard. At St James's Palace, there was a running and crying out of ladies and gentlemen, shutting of doors and windows. The voices of women and children were so great, it was heard at the top of the White Tower! [Whitehall] Also, the great shot was well discerned there from St James's fields. On the leads of St James's Palace stood anxious spectators. Wyatt went on to Ludgate, but his followers deserted him, and he was seized. His head was fixed to the Public Gallows at Hay Hill, from whence it was afterwards, stolen away.

This street is, of course, where King Charles II played his favourite game of Pell Mell. The course was moved to the Mall, then part of the Royal Estate, because of dust and the inconvenience of traffic on the road. An entry from the diary of Samuel Pepys from September 1661 tells us that 'This month, the road formerly used for all

5. (*above*) The Mall in 1750, showing the marker boards used by Charles II when playing 'Pell Mell', painted by H. Roberts.

6. (*left*) Portrait of Samuel Pepys by John Hayls, 1666.

coaches, carts and horses, from Charing Cross to St James's by St James's Park Wall, is now altered – by reason, a new Pell Mell is made for the use of his Majesty in the Park'. The dust from coaches had been very troublesome to the players at Mell. 'The new road railed on both sides, five foot distance the whole field length.' Pepys again, on 16 May 1664: 'I walked in the Park, discoursing with the keeper of the Pell Mell, who was sweeping of it, who told me of what the earth is mixed that do floor the Mell, and that overall, there is cockleshells pounded, spread to keep it fast, which, in dry weather, turns to dust and dead's the ball'.

The name comes from 'palla', a ball, and 'maglia', a mallet, and was a cross between golf and croquet. The mall was about half a mile long, with an arch or hoop at each end, and a border marked to show the position of the ball. Mallets were of different sizes to match the player, balls varied in weight according to the weather; if it was damp, making the soil heavy, a lighter ball was used. The mallet was lifted above the head and brought down with some force on the ball. This needed quite a lot of skill as there had to be some speed, yet the ball should not leave the ground but 'struck through an arch of iron at either end of the alley, in which he that can do, with the fewest blows, wins'.

7. Nell Gwynne's house, 1820.

8. Nell Gwynne, studio of Sir Peter Lely, c.1675.

By 1662-4 Henry Jermyn had begun his building programme, particularly St James's Square and its side streets (see pp. 41-53). Within a few years the Palace was no longer isolated. By 1690 Pall Mall was lined with buildings. A Mr. Lewis, writing to the historian Grainger on 7 March 1771, said: 'My friend, Doctor Heberden, has a fine house in Pall Mall, on the Palace side. He told me it was the only freehold on that side. It was given by a long lease, under the Crown by Charles II to Nell Gwynne. When she found it was only lease, she returned the lease and conveyance, saying she always conveyed free under the crown and always would, and would not accept until it was conveyed free to her by an Act of Parliament! Upon Nelly's death, it was sold and has been free ever since.' Nell Gwynne's house was number 79, and she lived there from 1671 to 1687. The house had a garden which abutted onto the park.

Charles II was a saunterer by nature, and appears to have been quite happy in the park, chatting to Nell at the end of the garden of her Pall Mall house, feeding the fowl, or playing at Mell. John Evelyn saw and heard a familiar discourse between the king and 'Mrs. Nellie'. She was looking out of her garden on a terrace at the top of the wall, and the king was standing on the green walk under it. Mrs. Mary Knight, another love, also lived on that side of the street; the Duchesse de Mazarin also, a lovely and eccentric mistress; the superb Barbara Castlemaine not far away in Cleveland House (now Bridgewater House). More will be said about Barbara Castlemaine in another chapter.

Wycherley, one of the bawdiest of Restoration playwrights, whose comedy *Love in a wood* is set in St James's Park, was walking along Pall Mall when Barbara Castlemaine drove past in her coach. Leaning out of the window she shouted 'Wycherley, you're the son of a whore'. Wycherley, no respecter of persons in his plays, thought this a compliment, followed her into the park and so began their affair. King Charles, always delighted by his plays, forgave their little indiscretion; indeed, he made Wycherley one of his many court equerries.

Daniel Defoe wrote in 1703:

> I am lodged in Pall Mall, the residence of all strangers, because of its vicinity to the Palace, the Park, Parliament, Theatres, Chocolate and Coffee Houses. About twelve o'clock, the *beau monde* assemble in several coffee houses, the best are the Cocoa Tree, Whites, St James's and The Smyrna. In less than an hour you see the company of all. We are carried in sedan-chairs, which are here very cheap – a guinea a week, or a shilling an hour – and your chairmen serve you as porters to run errands, as your gondoliers in Venice.

Now let us examine some of the houses and their residents. Schomberg House was built in the reign of William III for the Count of that name; Gainsborough, the famous painter, lived in the West Wing from 1777 until his death in 1788 (look for the blue plaque on the wall). At one time this house was part of the Foreign Office. Almost opposite there was the *Star and Garter* tavern; Swift wrote of drinking there on 30 March 1711. A club still existed within this tavern in 1763. The members were George Selwyn, Gilly Williams and their circle of wits. Lord Byron and Mr. Chaworth fought a famous duel here on 26 January 1765; Byron won, killing his opponent.

Carlton House was a scene of magnificent splendour when the Prince Regent lived there; this mansion, originally built for Lord Carlton in 1709, was bequeathed to his

9. Sedan chair stand in Whitehall, 1724.

10. (*above*) Carlton House, 1783.

11. (*right*) Schomberg House in 1820, from the *Pall Mall* magazine.

nephew, Lord Burlington, and bought by Frederick, Prince of Wales in 1732. It was built of red brick. In 1783 it was assigned to George, Prince of Wales, who asked Holland to enlarge the house. A Corinthian portico was also added, and a series of Ionic columns fronted Pall Mall. In one of the lodges lived 'Big Sam', a porter over seven feet tall. On the Pall Mall frontage there were two storeys, but the ground sloped downwards, so that on the south side, facing the park, there were three storeys. There was a bow-windowed bedroom for the prince, with a dressing room and 'hot-bathe closet' *en suite*. Walpole's opinion of the house was that 'It has an august simplicity that astonishes me'. On 19 June 1811, the prince gave a superb dinner to 2,000 guests. A stream, with gold and silver fish, flowed through a marble canal across the centre of the table.

When Regent Street was being created, the original plan was to drive the new thoroughfare from Regent's Park, downhill, to end at Carlton House, as the home of the Prince Regent, but the scheme was not completed. In 1827 the mansion was torn down, its columns were removed to the National Gallery, and many of the other fittings were taken to Buckingham Palace.

Newspapers give us a picture of the street in 1870:

The continuous series of clubs which form the chief feature of Pall Mall, stand in ground formerly occupied by Carlton House and its gardens, which stretched from Spring Gardens (near Admiralty Arch), to Marlborough House Gardens. The house had an entrance in St James's Park. The clubs are The Athenaeum, The Reform, The Travellers, The Carlton, The Oxford and Cambridge.

Pall Mall is the handsomest street in London, and when the War Office is rebuilt, its south side will be a continuous row of palaces. The north is following the lead of the south side, the Carlton Club is the latest edition. It now only wants to be opened up to Green Park, through Cleveland Row, to complete the grandeur.

This plan, like that for Regent Street, was never carried out.

Today Pall Mall has no 18th-century clubs left. Brook's and Boodle's, now in St James's Street, began life here. The Carlton Club was bombed out of existence in 1940.

Many famous London institutions were once housed in Pall Mall: at Number 49 was once Almack's Assembly Rooms, famous social venue of the late 18th and early 19th century; then the London Library, which moved to St James's Square in 1844; then it became Brook's Club, and it is now the headquarters of the British Legion. Number 52 was Dodsley's Bookshop, whose customers included Samuel Johnson and Horace Walpole; it later became the Marlborough Club, a favourite with Edward VII.

Number 64 was once the Jacobite Cocoa Tree Club (which also leased numbers 83 and 87 at different times). It is now Rothman's shop; in the early 16th century this was a lonely farmhouse. Number 81 was Payne's, a bookseller. Number 89 was a hatter's with a beautiful bay window. Number 100 was the first site of the National Gallery.

Number 79 is of special interest. Sir Thomas Clarges built a house here in 1664. (He had carried General Monck's letter to Charles II in exile, asking him to return as king, and was knighted on the spot.) He also owned the next house, and eventually

12.   Old houses in Pall Mall, *c.*1830.

13.   An unusually empty Mall, 7 a.m. on a Sunday in 1986. View from Buckingham Palace to Admiralty Arch.

sold the 'two brick messuages' to Sir William Coventry, who was often visited by Samuel Pepys. Eventually, Nell Gwynne moved from Cleveland Row into number 79 in 1671 and lived there until her death. Count Schomburg lived here, while his own house was being built, and finally Dr. Heberden rebuilt it in 1770. His comments on the house are recorded earlier in this chapter.

Thomas Christie, the world-famous auctioneer, started business in Pall Mall in 1766, opposite the old Opera House, which stood at the corner of Haymarket where New Zealand House now stands. In 1768 he leased numbers 83 and 84, and sublet to the painter, Gainsborough, to whom a stream of lovely ladies, including Perdita Robinson, an actress and the king's mistress, sat for their portraits. (This site was also to be the first home of the Cocoa Tree Club.) In the earliest days of art sales prices were ridiculously low, people bid much higher for horses. A Titian went for two guineas and a Lely for £8 7s. 6d. Christie's today do business in King Street.

In 1807 a modern miracle took place. Mr. F. A. Windsor lit one side of the street with gas lamps on the king's birthday, 4 June, producing 'brilliant illumination' of the full length between Pall Mall and St James's Park. Gas lamps continue in use at St James's Palace in 1987, the soft light enhancing the beauty of the scene.

St James's Street

Prior to 1531 this street was a lane, running uphill from the Convent where the Palace now stands, to the 'road to Knyghtsbridge and Reading', as Piccadilly was then known. According to the rate books for 1599 only Mrs. Anne Poultney and Mr. Baldwin were residents, probably at the farmhouse where Rothman's shop stands today, with gates opening on to the lane through the hedges.

In 1532, when Henry VIII built a hunting lodge, he drove down this lane with Anne Boleyn, taking her away from the scandalised, gossiping court at the Palace of Westminster.

When Charles II returned from exile in 1660, the glittering Stuart court moved into the Palace, creating an urgent need to house court officials, merchants and inns. St James's Street and Square quickly gained many elegant buildings and became the centre of social, political and intellectual life for many years to come.

Eighteenth-century streets were dark; the only light came from oil lamps with smoky fumes which hung over doors on moonless nights. The kennel, a deep ditch in the middle of the road, stank, running with every kind of filth. Women wore wooden pattens to protect their feet, and the mud was cleaned several times a day from the men's highly-polished knee boots. There was continuous noise from the rattle of wooden wheels over cobble stones: the luxurious coaches of the

14. Portrait of Anne Boleyn by an unknown artist.

nobility; the public hackney coaches with their foul-mouthed drivers. Sedan chairs, however, were the most common form of transport. They were carried by porters, often drunk. All these vehicles drove pedestrians to the wall. Nobles and gentry rode from their beautiful houses and never walked if they could avoid it.

There was noise also from many creaking iron signs with elaborately-gilded designs, as houses were not numbered. Noise from street pedlars' cries – 'Cherries, ripe cherries', 'Mend your pots and pans', 'Milko', 'Laces and pretty pins', 'Oysters, shilling a peck'; and newspaper boys – the first daily, *The Daily Courant*, was published in 1702.

Yet within the great houses life was gentle, full of lovely possessions, and social niceties were of great importance. The sole survivor today of those great aristocratic

15. Milkmaids, painted by F. Wheatley.

16. 'Live Haddock', published 1815.

17. The Peddler.

18. The Rabbit Woman, published 1805.

and political houses of 18th-century London is Spencer House at the far end of St James's Place, built by Lord Spencer, ancestor of our present Princess of Wales, in 1760.

The famous clubs of St James's all began as chocolate and coffee houses. When cocoa and coffee beans were discovered in the New World, and brought to London, these houses sprang up everywhere as meeting places to drink, gossip, read the news-sheets and do business. Berry Brothers and Rudd, at 3 St James's Street, sold these beans and other exotic things from overseas to those new establishments. (More will be said about this shop's fascinating history on pp. 35-38.)

Another famous shop, Fortnum and Mason, was founded in 1707. Mason ran a small shop in St James's Market, and Fortnum lodged with him and became a footman at the Palace, with the perquisite of all the half-burnt candles (of which there would have been hundreds). They became partners, selling the candles, but later capitalised on Mr. Fortnum's knowledge of Queen Anne's fondness for a dish of 'tay' and laid the basis of Fortnum and Mason's early reputation.

As time passed each club tended to become identified with a particular political or social grouping, reflected in the contemporary joke about a young man of fashion, who said 'At about twelve o'clock I go to the Cocoa Tree where I talk treason; then to St James's Coffee House, where I praise the Ministry; thence to Whites where I talk of gallantry'. A writer in 1847 said 'It is remarkable that of two of the old chocolate houses, the Cocoa Tree and White's, only White's has acquired a second youth. The Cocoa Tree was the favourite resort of George IV when still Prince of Wales, and it only ceased to exist in the last few years. It was the meeting place for the Jacobites, Tories, Wits and Dandies in Queen Anne's reign.' This observation is confirmed by Daniel Defoe, who wrote that 'A Whig would no more go to the Cocoa Tree than a Tory would be seen at the St James's Coffee House'.

19. Portrait of George IV by Sir Thomas Lawrence, c.1814.

White's is shown in Hogarth's 'Rake's Progress'. The members are so absorbed in gambling they are unaware the club is on fire! Horace Walpole wrote in September 1750 of a story about White's in the papers: 'A man dropped dead at the door and was carried in; the club immediately made bets whether he was dead or not. When they were going to 'bleed' him, the wagerers interposed, said it would affect the fairness of the bet.'

Brook's, a Whig stronghold, opened in 1778 and was originally in Pall Mall, near what was later to be the site of the Marlborough Club. Edward VII formed this club

20. (*above*) 'The Rake's Progress' by Hogarth, showing the interior of White's Chocolate House before 1733.

21. (*below*) 'Promised Horrors of the French Invasion, shewing White's and Brookes's', from the caricature by Gillray, published in 1796.

22. (*right*) William Hogarth, self portrait, *c.*1757.

23. (*below*) 'The Rake's Progress', by Hogarth: arrested for debt on his way to court.

24. The exterior of White's Club.

25. St James's Street in 1750, with Boodle's Club on the left.

26. 'Making a Member.'

27. Engraving of the Great Subscription Room at Brook's Club by Rowlandson, c. 1810.

28. Berry Bros. and Rudd,
18th-century wine merchants.

29. Lock's, 18th-century hatter.

in 1872, opposite Marlborough House, when he found smoking cigars in White's severely restricted. He made the rule that smoking be allowed everywhere in the Marlborough, except the Dining Room.

Charles James Fox lived in a house near Brook's in 1781. Walpole said: 'Fox, who in his later years became slovenly, was, when young, one of the greatest swells; Beau Fox was to be seen strutting down St James's Street in a suit of french embroidery, a little silk hat, red heeled shoes and a bouquet large enough for a maypole!'.

Boodle's Club was designed in the style of Robert Adams and is the only building in London attributed to Crunden. Essentially the same today as it was in 1765, it is a beautiful building and a sense of the past still comes from a stroll past White's at number 37, Brook's at number 60, the Carlton at number 69, and Boodle's at number 28. Then on to the shops: Berry Brothers and Rudd at number 3, Locks the Hatters at number 6, and Lobb's the Bootmakers at number 9.

Lock's success began from the patronage of the old Whig families of Marlborough, Bedford, Devonshire and Walpole. Later, James Lock realised the potential of supplying head-gear to the Army and Navy. The firm made the hat that Nelson wore at the Battle of Trafalgar; also the ornately-plumed hat worn by Wellington at the Battle of Waterloo!

As in Pall Mall, property has changed hands, or been rebuilt, many times. We can remember the crowds outside Miss Humphries' print shop at number 29, jostling to see the latest satirical cartoons by Gillray when we pass today's Harris' the Chemist at the same address.

30. Portrait of James Gillray, attributed to himself, *c*.1800.

31. Portrait of Jonathan Swift, by Charles Jervas, *c*.1718.

Jonathan Swift was often to be seen in St James's Street. He appears to have changed his lodgings frequently and attended many clubs and coffee houses here, always writing his 'Letters to Stella', which give us such a clear picture of life in St James's.

At number 62 Elizabeth Neale was born. She ran Betty's Fruit Shop, where everyone came to lounge and gossip. Betty knew all the social and political scandal; she lived here from 1730, retiring in 1783 to Park Place where she lived until her death in 1797. She only slept away from home twice in her life. At numbers 27-28 lived Banting, the hugely obese undertaker and upholsterer, whose method of slimming added the now obsolete term 'banting' to the language. William Banting (1797-1878) was aged 66 and over 14 stone when he began to deny himself bread, butter, milk, sugar, beer, soup, potatoes and beans. Instead he ate meat, fish and dry toast.As a result, he lost three stone in weight and 12½ inches round the waist.

At the top of the street, in Piccadilly, once stood the mansion of the Earl of Clarendon, then the Lord Chancellor, exactly opposite the Palace. John Evelyn's diary has an entry in October 1664: 'After dinner, my Lord Chancellor and his Lady, carried me in their coach to see their Palace at the upper end of St James's Street'. Two years earlier, in 1662, he had noted that work was in hand 'paving the way north of the Palace'. We may wonder if the work was completed by 1664. It would have made travel between the king in his palace at the bottom of the hill, and the Chancellor in his mansion at the top, so much easier.

There have been many inns of great character in St James's Street in the past, all sadly vanished. Walking downhill, just after Park Place, one can see Blue Ball Yard on the right. This gives an instant 'feel' of an 18th-century inn stableyard. At one

32. Victorian view of the south end of St James's Street, showing the new club house and the Palace.

time Jermyn Street was a cul-de-sac, because an inn, the *King's Head* next to White's, lay across the present intersection with St James's Street. When that inn was demolished it was the attached stableyard which made access a simple matter.

This street has seen attempted rebellion, the Prince Regent and Beau Brummel 'cut' one another, Dr. Johnson buying shoe buckles at Wirgman's; Swift, Pope, Waller and Byron at number 8; the artist, James Gillray, who threw himself to his death from an upper window in 1815; the historian, Edward Gibbon, who died at number 76; Sir Christopher Wren, who died in his bed in lodgings in 1725, aged 91; and Captain Blood's attempt to kidnap the Duke of Ormonde – the same Blood who almost succeeded in stealing the Crown Jewels.

33. Relief of Charles II and Jermyn on the corner of Jermyn Street and Bury Street: Charles hands over the title to the land.

Jermyn Street

Henry Jermyn, Earl of St Albans, man of many talents, was Ambassador to France during the reign of Charles I, and eventually Vice Chancellor to Queen Henrietta Maria. During the long years of Charles II's exile Jermyn managed the Queen's Privy Purse. Upon restoration in 1660, Charles created him Lord High Admiral; and with much assistance from royal gratitude for his loyalty he became immensely rich.

He loved gambling, women, good food, and possessed a flair for successful opportunism, including building speculation. Having built, in 1662, the 'great and good' houses in St James's Square for people of consequence and for court officials (see pp. 31-34), he turned his attention in 1667 to Jermyn Street, to the construction of the small shops and houses providing services and tradesmen for the needs of that elegant square.

Royal Letters-Patent, permitting the building work to commence, were issued on 31 May 1682 by Charles II, allowing the construction of the church to begin. It was originally meant to front Jermyn Street, at that time of much greater importance than Piccadilly. Wheatley tells us in 1872: 'There used to be a fine door opposite Duke of York Street (this leads into the Square), which was blocked up in 1856, but the gate in the railings remains to show its position'.

The church was intended for the use of eminent residents, who paid dearly for the privilege. Daniel Defoe was horrified by the exorbitant charges for a pew. He said, 'It costs one almost as dear to see a play'. But if you lived in the Square, as did Jermyn, this exclusive social ambit was part of your life. John Evelyn's diary for 7 December 1684, says: 'I went to see the new Church of St James's – very elegant'. The church was badly damaged by bombing in World War II, in 1940; it has since been beautifully restored by Sir Albert Richardson, with the loving care of dedicated craftsmen.

Jermyn Street was a street of hotels. The *Gun Tavern* was one, and *Rouelles* and *Greniere* were both noted for their foreign guests, especially during the French Revolution, when many emigrés centred upon the *Hotel Greniere*. Perhaps the most famous hotel in this area, however, was the *Cavendish* (see p. 51). Some of the well-known residents of Jermyn Street have included the elder Pitt in 1763; Sidney Smith at number 81 in 1811; Thomas Moore at number 58 in 1825; and Gladstone in 1832, when he first entered Parliament (he lodged in rooms over Cramperns, the corn merchant). Lord Nelson also lodged here, as did Colonel Churchill, the future Duke of Marlborough, in his early bachelor days; Isaac Newton, from 1697 to 1709, lived in a house near the church. Sheridan was here in 1793, and the poet, Thomas Gray, lived here in 1753. He said, 'I won't give more than half-a-guinea, nor put up with the second floor, unless it has a tolerable room to the street'. He was either at Robert's the hosiers, or Frisby the oilman at the eastern end. Sir Walter Scott stayed at St James's Hotel, number 76.

St James's Market, which used to lie between the Square and the Haymarket, dealt in fresh meat, vegetables, etc. until Lower Regent Street was built by Nash to lead

34. St James's church, Jermyn Street.

35. Portrait of John Evelyn, by Robert Walker, 1648.

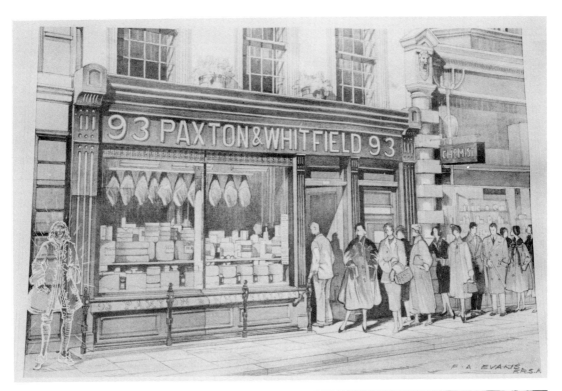

36. (*above*) Paxton & Whitfield (1781),
Jermyn Street: 'We seemed to have a
ghost in the early 1950s'.

37. (*right*) Floris shop (1730) in Jermyn
Street, 1986.

to the prince's house in Pall Mall, sweeping the old market away for ever. Jermyn Street today is still a magnet for shoppers, but for exquisite luxury goods and fine foods.

Paxton and Whitfield, the world-famous cheesemongers, whose earlier history lies elsewhere in London, first started their business in Jermyn Street at number 18, but eventually settled at number 93 in 1781, where they still do business today in their original 18th-century shop. Some concessions to modern requirements have been made – as few as possible; and most certainly not in the quality of the cheese, for which many visitors and many more Londoners show deep appreciation. Do not forget to experience this special place. Rosa Lewis (the 'Duchess of Duke Street') used this shop for many of her requirements for the *Cavendish* Hotel.

Rosa was probably a constant customer at number 89, Floris, yet another absolute jewel among these old St James's shops, founded in the 18th century. Juan Floris was a Minorcan, who came to London in 1730 to start his business life as a perfumier. His family, seven generations later, carry on the business today, with that old-world courtesy so typical of St James's.

Floris' had become, by 1800, comb-makers to her Royal Highness, the Princess of Wales; beautiful inlaid tortoise-shell hairpins and combs. But always there were those glorious perfumes, essences and soaps for which Floris' still remain famous, world-wide. The shop front is the original, and its show cases date from 1850: how lucky that it escaped the devastation suffered by the church and many other neighbouring buildings during the air-raids of 1940.

A sad loss to the whole of St James's was the Hammam, or Turkish Bath, opened in 1862 at number 76, 'which cost £6,000 to build, of eastern architecture', and which closed amidst protests only a few years ago. It seemed an integral part of this man's world, where the English gentleman can still stroll to his shirtmaker or wine and cigar merchant, consider antiques and old masters, visit his tailor, hatter, barber or shoemaker – all within a short distance of his club. Truly a smooth, purring, exclusively male preserve, quite unlike anywhere else in the world. Henry VIII, and indeed, Charles II, would have greatly appreciated all that Jermyn Street offers.

St James's Square

This beautiful square was built in 1663, also by Henry Jermyn, Earl of St Albans. A Warrant was issued to Baptist May and Abraham Cowley on the nomination of Jermyn of 'several parcels of ground in Pall Mall, at a cost of eighty shillings, for building a square of thirteen or fourteen great and good houses'. It was intended exclusively for the nobles and courtiers in positions of power in attendance upon King Charles II, after the restoration of the Monarchy. An historian of 1766 tells us how it looked a century later:

> It is neatly paved with heading-stone, in which there is a most curious oval basin, 150 feet in diameter, filled with water; in the centre is a pedestal, fifteen feet square, for a statue of William III on horseback. The whole is invironed with iron rails of eight feet square, at each angle without the rails, is a stone pillar about nine feet high, with a lamp on the top, and a gravel walk within the rails.

A writer of 1870 gives a rather different picture:

> St James's Square was a receptacle for all the offal, cinders, dead cats and dogs of Westminster. An impudent squatter built a shed under the windows of the gilded salons. It was not until these mansions had lasted a generation and much written about them, that Parliament gave permission to put up rails and plant trees. In February 1725-6, residents petitioned to be allowed to cleanse and adorn the Square. In 1727 a basin of water was opened with a pleasure boat and railing. [This remained for about 100 years, and was filled in after 1870.] The South Side has always been of little account, and is vastly improved by the new Carlton Club.

Here lived James II's mistress, Catherine Sedley. When they parted, the king created her Baroness Darlington and Countess of Dorchester, and gave her a house, number 21, for her well-earned retirement. A social reporter said: 'She retired from the embraces of her Royal lover with a coronet, a house and a pew in the Church'.

Another resident was Mrs. Davies, the actress, who left the stage to become one of the endless list of Charles II's mistresses. The Duke of Ormonde, who fought for Charles I and followed Charles II into exile, had a house on the north side. We are told that 'Duke of York Street comes out of St James's Square, a broad street, but the greatest part is the garden wall of the Duke of Ormonde'.

Frances, Duchess of Richmond, lived at number 15, but before her marriage she was La Belle Stewart, that icily chaste and utterly beautiful girl, constant in her refusals to Charles II. Also resident in the square was the Earl of Northumberland, Charles II's son by the Duchess of Cleveland, and Lady Suffolk, George II's mistress. A century later Lady Betty Germaine was hostess to the Prince of Wales at number 16 when despatches arrived on 20 June 1815 with news of the victory at Waterloo two days earlier.

At number 14, at the north-west corner of the square, lived Sir Philip Francis, who died in 1818. In 1820 Queen Caroline became a short-stay tenant during her trial by the House of Lords, driving in state to Parliament each day, whilst she defended her

38. St James's Square in 1754 with a boat on the pond.

39. St James's Square in 1812.

40. London Library, No. 14 St James's Square, in 1986.

41. Portrait of Frederick Lewis, Prince of Wales, by Philip Mercier, c.1736.

42. Memorial to the policewoman killed in the Libyan Embassy siege, 1984.

43. The shuttered and empty Libyan Embassy opposite the memorial, 1986.

right to royal status which her husband, George IV, was attempting to nullify. The London Library is there today, having moved from Pall Mall in 1844, a magnificent and quite unique institution.

Frederick, Prince of Wales, lived at number 21 while Carlton House in Pall Mall was being altered for him. This was the Duke of Norfolk's house and the present building on the site is today known as Norfolk House. Yet another royal mistress, Arabella Churchill, the Duke of Marlborough's sister, lived in this square; James, Duke of York, insisted she reside near the Palace during his short-lived passion for the lady.

Other residents at different times have included William Pitt the Younger, Warren Hastings and Sir Robert Walpole among many other politicians. Josiah Wedgwood of the Pottery firm lived at number 7 and at number 4, Earl Grey. Lord Hervey lived at number 6, and was in constant attention upon Queen Caroline. At number 17 lived the Duke of Cleveland, where hung a picture by Lely of the Duchess of Cleveland, Charles II's stormy mistress.

In recent years the Astor family owned a house here, and during World War II General Eisenhower had his London base here, as did General de Gaulle. Although the facades of the houses show no sign of it, some still contain 17th-century interior decoration.

On 17 April 1984 the peace of this beautiful square was horribly shattered. On the north-east corner of St James's Square, a few hundred yards away from the Palace, is the former Libyan Embassy, now described as the 'Headquarters of the People's Republic of Libya'. A small, peaceful demonstration by a group of students was in progress, by the still stately front entrance, accompanied by the normal police attendance. Suddenly an embassy window opened, a machine gun was thrust out, and students, passers-by and police were fired upon indiscriminately. A policewoman died. Her murderer's identity has never been discovered, but her tragic death is recorded for posterity by a simple, dignified memorial.

Pickering Place

This is an enchanting 18th-century courtyard, the absolute essence of old St James's. You will find it at the end of a narrow, oak-lined passage by number 3 St James's Street – Berry Brothers & Rudd. Norden, Elizabeth I's Surveyor of Building, wrote in 1598 that 'The Palace standeth from other buildings, saving a farme opposite its north gate', that is, on this site. Sixty years later Faithorne's map of 1658 shows three buildings only on this corner; the whole hillside was still farmland.

In 1664 a petition was submitted to the king for 'leave to convey water to nine residents'. By 1691 there were 28 residents of St James's Street. Thomas Stroud had built a courtyard and houses by 1695, and was a registered rate-payer. By 1705 William Pickering (yearly rates £1 6s. 8d.) and Mrs. Stroud (rates £2), were the residents.

A building agreement was made by Pickering in 1731 to erect: 'on the parcel of ground known formerly as St James's Field, now known as Stroud's Court, two dwelling houses on the front, facing the street, leaving a passage to the back houses'. This is the building known today as Berry Brothers & Rudd, number 3 St James's Street. He agreed further 'to build two or more houses on the east' – these are number 1, 2, 3 and 4 in Pickering Place, within the courtyard.

Originally Berry Bros. was a grocery, selling coffee and chocolate, tobacco and spices, all discovered in the New World of the Americas. The sign over the door said 'The Coffee Mill', and they supplied all the coffee and chocolate houses springing up in St James's. In 1756 they began the tradition of weighing eminent customers on their great scales which were balanced by huge beams in the shop ceiling, and by 1765 ledgers were kept, daily recording the weight of these celebrities. Among those listed are the royal Dukes of York, Clarence and Cumberland, Charles James Fox, George Selwyn the 18th-century wit, Beau Nash, Byron, Creevy the gossip, Lord Melbourne, Queen Victoria's first Prime Minister, and Sir Robert Peel, founder of the Metropolitan Police. It became the fashionable thing, to gossip and watch your friends being weighed!

44. Portrait of Charles James Fox, by K. A. Hickel.

45. Typical 18th-century houses in Pickering Place.

46. An 18th-century courtyard: the passage by Berry Bros. and Rudd.

In 1756 John Clark became a partner in the business and by 1803 his grandson, John Berry, had entered the firm. In 1896 the groceries were sold off, and from that date only wine has been sold here. Major Rudd added his name to this famous establishment in 1918.

The secluded courtyard was perfect for illicit pastimes – one advertisement read 'Pickering Place – Rouge and Roulette' – at the time it was well known as a gambling hell. Duels were fought here. After the Metropolitan Police were formed in 1829, those wishing to carry on outlawed activities found life becoming difficult. 'Swords for two in the park' became an impossibility, but in Pickering Place, with a look-out outside the passage, they proceeded to kill each other in privacy. Who fought the last duel? Writers of the early 19th century mention fights but, as secrecy was the essential thing, no names!

One final point of interest: on the right hand wall at the inner end of the oak-lined passage is a single star, marking the existence here of the Texan Embassy during the time of that State's Independence.

Cleveland Row

This street faces St James's Palace, and is so called from Cleveland House, which once stood on the site of the present Bridgewater House (see p. 79). A topographer noted in 1840: The houses on the north side of Cleveland Row are the originals from Queen Anne's reign'. Colonel John Selwyn, aide-de-camp to the Duke of Marlborough, lived in one of them with his son, George. Nearby lived George's great friend and correspondent for 20 years, Gilly Williams. At number 5 lived Theodore Hook, a playwright and novelist. George, Gilly and Theodore formed a trio, famous for witticisms and practical jokes.

Poets also lived here: William Mason wrote to Thomas Grey on 2 February 1767 that 'We are to be found at Mr Mennis, a Tailor, near the Golden Ball in Cleveland Row, the last door but one nearest the Green Park wall'. There was by that date a

47. The corner of Cleveland Row and St James's Street (right), opposite the Palace.

48. The end of Cleveland Row: the corner with Stable Yard, where George III's drunken coach driver overturned.

longer row of houses on both sides at the western end, with the mansion behind in a courtyard.

Sir Edward Hertslet wrote in May 1763 that 'The Earl of Bute has removed the Foreign Office from Whitehall, to a house in Cleveland Row'. And Nell Gwynne lived here in a tiny house, quite close to Green Park, before Charles II bought for her a much larger establishment in Pall Mall.

King Street

This street was built in 1673. Even in 1686 it was still referred to as being 'in the fields', so long had this area remained farmland. Almack's Assembly Rooms opened on the south side in 1765; Gilly Williams wrote to George Selwyn on 12 February that year that: 'At Almach's, in three very elegant new rooms, a ten-guinea subscription for which you have a ball and supper once a week for ten weeks. Old Almack's Scottish face in a bag-wig, waiting at supper would divert you, as would his lady in

49.   King Street in 1986, looking towards the Square.

50.   Christie's in King Street, 1986.

a sack, making tea and curtseying to the Duchesses'. The average attendance was 1,700. Despite its apparently insipid entertainment, admission to Almack's conferred the ultimate social cachet, and was for many years essential for anyone wanting to make their way in society.

Christie's, the art auctioneers, who began their business life in Pall Mall in 1766, moved here in 1823.

Bury Street

51. Bury Street in 1986, looking from King Street to Jermyn Street.

Colonel Bury, who had served in Charles I's army, built Bury Street in 1672, and lived here as resident landlord until his death, aged 101 years. Jonathan Swift lodged here in 1810, and wrote to his beloved Stella in September: 'I have the first floor, a dining room and a bed-chamber at eight shillings a week; Plaguey dear, but I spend nothing for eating, never go to a tavern and seldom in a coach, yet after all it will be expensive'.

Little St James's Street

52.   The back elevation of *Duke's Hotel* in 1986.

Mrs. Delaney, a long-term resident of St James's Palace, once took a house here. In a letter to her sister on 14 October 1768 she describes it as 'a house behind the Thatched House Tavern in St James's Street near Catherine-Wheel Lane. The front faces Little St James's Street, and the back looks into the Duke of Bridgewater's garden very pleasantly'.

Blue Ball Yard

53. Blue Ball Yard.

This is one of the very few places where one gets the true feeling of an 18th-century stableyard. It lies north of St James's Place, and obviously in the past lay behind an inn.

54. Entrance to Blue Ball Yard.

Park Place

In the 18th century this was the site of an infamous brothel. Mother Needham was the madame at this house of joy, commemorated by Hogarth with a bitter caricature, in plate 1 of his series 'The Rake's Progress'. In *Fogg's Weekly Journal* for 1 May 1731 it was reported that 'The noted Mother Needham convicted April 20, 1731 for keeping a disorderly house in Park Place, St James's, was fined one shilling and had

55. Park Place in 1986. The stocks were once sited on the right hand side of the street.

to stand twice in the pillory, once in St James's over against the end of Park Place, and once in New Palace Yard, Westminster, and to find sureties for her good behaviour for three years'. The *Grub Street Journal* on 7 May 1731 stated that 'Yesterday, the noted Mother Needham stood in the pillory by Park Place, and was roughly handled by the populace'. One can well imagine the old harridan, held in the wooden frame by her neck and wrists, possibly by the feet, pelted with rotten fruit by every passer-by, not to mention her neighbours.

Arlington Street

This street was built by Lord Arlington in 1681, and almost all the residents were of the aristocracy. The lords Brook, Cholmondeley, Guildford, Peterborough and Kingston lived here, as did Barbara, Duchess of Cleveland, who found it too expensive to remain in Cleveland House after Charles II's death and lived here from 1691 until 1696.

Sir Robert Walpole, the Prime Minister, was a resident for 13 years, until his death in 1746. His son, Horace Walpole, was born here in 1717, and continued to live here after his father's death until 1779. He wrote 'nothing could be more dignified. Arlington has been the ministerial street from my earliest memory'. George II, when still Prince of Wales, stayed here after one of his many celebrated quarrels with his father, who requested he leave the palace. The Duke of Cumberland, the 'Butcher of Culloden', dined here on the night he died.

56. Portrait of Horace Walpole, 4th Earl of Orford, by J. G. Eccardt, 1754.

57. Walpole's house in Arlington Street, second from the right.

J. H. BOURDON-SMITH LTD.
Antique Silver   Antique Silver
24 MASONS YARD   THROUGH ARCHWAY

58. Mason's Yard, off Duke Street: the rear entrance to Rosa Lewis's *Cavendish Hotel*.

Duke Street

Duke Street was the first street in London to be paved to modern standards. In the 18th century the Duke of Shrewsbury had a house and garden here. Jonathan Swift, who moved about the St James's area with some regularity, also lodged here. He wrote in July 1717: 'When you come to London, do not go to The Cocoa Tree, but come to Duke Street, where you shall find a bed, a book and a candle'. This was one of the tradesmen's areas which supplied the residents of the Square – small houses, bakeries and shops; as was Mason's Yard.

The most famous building on the corner of this street is, of course, the *Cavendish* Hotel, with its memories of Rosa Lewis – although, to be strictly honest, it is really on the *corner* of Duke and Jermyn Streets. Nevertheless, the recent television series has made Rosa famous as the 'Duchess of Duke Street' and for that reason her story is told here. Rosa was born Rosa Ovenden and came from Leyton, in London. She was a lovely golden girl with blue eyes, a certain panache, a brilliant cook and business woman. She had a strong personality which became domineering in her later years. In her first post within the household of the Count de Paris, she learnt the routine of an aristocratic house with a large staff. It was here that she first met Edward VII, a lifelong friend (and perhaps lover), when he came to dinner: he always appreciated superb food and wine.

She then started her own catering business for social occasions: she would bring her own staff and prepare a meal in her client's home. She began importing Virginia hams to cook for Mr. Jackson of Piccadilly, and it was Jackson who told her of the hotel (which dated from 1674) for sale in Jermyn Street.

Having bought the end of the lease, it was fully transferred to her in 1904, whereupon she both extended and modernised the hotel. The *Cavendish* was not for just anyone. Were you *persona non grata*, the doors were closed; for the favoured but discreet, Mason's Yard gave entry at the rear of the hotel from a pleasant little courtyard – you could bring your lady friend in and avoid the busy eyes at the front entrance.

For 50 years Rosa was a benevolent autocrat, managing what amounted to a private club. The visitors' book was solid with exalted names, champagne flowed, and a single room cost 8s. 6d., a full breakfast 3s. 6d., and dinner 7s. 6d. In the Second World War Richard Hillary, a Fighter Command pilot wrote:

> One night in town we went to see Rosa Lewis at the Cavendish. Caught by a stroke, she had been rushed to the London Clinic where she refused to allow the nurses to touch her. After a week, she saw the bill, got up and left. When we arrived, there she was, 76 years old, shrieking with laughter and waving a glass of champagne, apparently none the worse. She grabbed me by the arm, peered into my face "God, aren't you dead yet, either, young Hillary? Come here and I'll tell you something. Don't you ever die. In the last two weeks I've been right up to the gates of 'eaven and 'ell and they're both bloody". Ten weeks later, a heavy bomb landed right on The Cavendish, but Rosa emerged triumphant, pulling pieces of glass out of her hair and trumpeting with rage. Whatever else may go in this war, we shall have Rosa Lewis and the Albert Memorial to the end.

Today's tall *Cavendish* Hotel would most certainly have had Rosa's approval – particularly the compliment paid by the 'Sub-Rosa' Bar, and the worn brass name-plates of her old hotel, still lovingly kept behind glass at each side of the entrance.

59. (*above*) Duke of York Street in 1986, from Jermyn Street to the Square.

60. (*below*) Charles Street from the Square in 1986, showing the Haymarket Theatre.
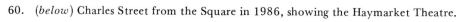

Duke of York Street

61. Duke of York Street in 1932, showing the trees in St James's Square at the bottom and Ormonde Yard to the right.
(Note: Ormonde should correctly be spelt with the final 'e'.)

When Jermyn built St James's Square in 1662, there had to be access roads on the east, the west and the north sides. (The south side had two short entrances to Pall Mall – John Street and James's Street, the shortest streets in London, now part of the Square.) The eastern exit was named Charles Street for the king, as was King Street on the west. The northern exit was named for the king's brother, later James II.

The Duke of Ormonde's house on the north of the square had a long garden running up to Jermyn Street, along the full length of Duke of York Street. Ormonde must have been happy in his lovely garden in the peaceful days of the Restoration.

Ormonde Yard

62. Ormonde Yard in 1986.
63. Apple Tree Yard (sometimes Orchard Yard) in 1986.

Ormonde Yard and Apple Tree Yard open off the Duke of York Street; Ormonde Yard was clearly his stable entrance – Apple Tree could well have been his orchard, but the whole of the area lying between Pall Mall and Piccadilly was famous for its apple trees long before any buildings appeared on the hill. The produce probably appeared in the Palace storeroom.

54

St James's Place

This street has always been known as an artist's haunt. It was built in 1694 and has the oddest mushroom shape – it starts as a simple street but opens out into a distorted cul-de-sac with three small courtyards. When one first enters from St James's Street there are houses on each side, facing the street, but as one nears Green Park there were originally eight or nine houses which turned their backs – the front facades looking onto the Park, the rears, with tiny gardens, facing St James's Place. These houses were much sought after.

All the land running uphill from the Palace on the left hand side of St James's Street, including St James's Place, is still Crown property today. To discover why, we must go back to 1665, to Charles II and his mistress, the Duchess of Cleveland. She lived in Cleveland House, today called Bridgewater House, close to the Palace, and her gardens ran north, almost up to the line of Piccadilly. Her stable-yard would have been entered from St James's Street; the stables were on the site of today's luxurious *Duke's* Hotel.

When the Duchess sold her land to pay huge gambling debts, her old stable-yard became a courtyard of small houses, pulled down 90 years ago to create today's charming hotel with its courtyard. Now we know why Charles II gave land to Henry Jermyn on the *right* side of the hill; the left hand side belonged to his mistress, and remains Crown Land today.

64. Portrait of Barbara Palmer, Duchess of Cleveland, by John Michael Wright, 1672.

The Place, St James's, was part of the Stuart building boom. By 1695, 11 residents were entered on the ancient Rate Books, and artists and playwrights have always been much in evidence. Congreve and Wycherley, the Restoration playwrights, often attended parties here, probably in Lord Godolphin's house.

William Cleland, in 1739, gave directions in a letter to his prospective visitor: 'walk up St James's Place as far as you can, keeping always to the right, then into a little courtyard, the centre door is mine'. In this second courtyard is the dignified and elegant *Stafford* Hotel which, like *Duke's* Hotel, enjoys discreet privacy.

Addison lived in 'The Place' in 1710, and John Wilks in 1756 'lodged elegantly at Mrs Murray's'. In 1747 Lady Harvey lived in a house overlooking the park. After some rebuilding she wrote to a friend in 1749: 'if I had made a bow window, I should have looked into Sir John Cope's rooms, and he into mine'. She was a beautiful

65. *Duke's* Hotel, 1986.   66. *Stafford* Hotel, 1986.

woman, with many distinguished friends, among them the poets Pope and Gay, both of whom wrote poems in praise of her.

On Lady Harvey's death in September 1768, Lord Carlisle moved into her house. He wrote to a friend in October 'I agree, it is very extravagant to give £200 a year to see a cow under my window, but I am very happy to have the house and hope you will like the present occupier as you did the last'. The cows were grazed in Green Park, and driven in to the Palace stable yard through Milkmaid's Passage, to be milked for the needs of the Palace.

Spencer House, on the left hand side of the 'mushroom cap', was built by the first Lord Spencer, replacing three or four of the original small houses. There was a great deal of social intercourse between the Spencers, Harveys and Copes, with that inveterate gossip Horace Walpole much in evidence.

67. (*above*) Spencer House in 1763: an engraving by
T. Miller.

68. (*right*) Houses opposite Spencer House, 1986.

69. Portrait of Fanny Burney (Frances d'Arblay), by Edward Francis Burney.

70. Oscar Wilde: a photograph by Napoleon Sarony, 1882.

71. Portrait of Samuel Rogers, by T. Phillips.

72. Samuel Rogers's house, backing on to St James's Place and facing Queen's Walk, 1845.

The artistic Mrs. Delaney lived in St James's Place from 1771 to 1788; an entrancing person, and an intimate in the domestic life of George III and Queen Charlotte, who came here to visit, to see her famous flower collages and silhouettes, many of the royal children.

In 1780 Charles James Fox, brilliant politician, lodged here. Mrs. Robinson, 'Perdita', George, Prince of Wales's mistress, lived at number 13. Samuel Rogers owned number 22 from 1803 until his death in 1855 in one of the houses overlooking the park.

He was immensely rich, his house beautifully furnished; he possessed many famous art treasures and spent his long years of residence here entertaining a brilliant circle of friends – breakfast being particularly favoured. Macaulay, Sheridan, Southey, Coleridge, Byron, Wordsworth, Fanny Burney – all came eagerly to 'breakfast at 10.00 a.m., when so agreeable and fascinating was the conversation, the repast seldom ended before 1 p.m.'. Tourists in London hovered at the door to catch a glimpse of the famous, even after Sam's death in 1855.

Rogers' house was 'by the convenient passage into Green Park', he said; and you can go through that passage today, only now it has become a tunnel beneath an apartment building, one of the many modern blocks, which so sadly bully St James's Place. The passage to the park was just a tiny country path, running alongside his house and garden, but from St James's Street it saves one walking either north or south on a circular route to reach the park and Queen's Walk, which in Rogers' day was a place of fashionable promenades.

The famous composer, Chopin, stayed in St James's Place when in London – indeed, he was in residence here for the last concert given during his lifetime. Look for the blue plaque on the house wall. Oscar Wilde leased number 10 for six months in 1893 and wrote his brilliant play 'An Ideal Husband' in strict seclusion; and in 1931 Sir Edward Elgar, famous English composer, stayed in one of the *Duke's* Hotel's private apartments when in London for concerts. Certainly, a street of artists.

St James's Park

This was the first royal park in London. We owe its beauty to Henry VIII, who drained and enclosed it when he built St James's Palace; to Charles II, who laid down avenues, planted trees and stocked it with wildlife; and to George IV who made more improvements in 1827, and in 1829 opened it to the public. Originally it was only a marshy meadow; once drained and cared for it became a great pleasure to residents of the Palace. Long before his son had laid the foundations of the park we love today, Charles I knew it well enough to point out a certain tree on that day he walked across from St James's Palace to the scaffold in Whitehall, on 30 January 1649.

During the years of the Commonwealth, Oliver Cromwell was seen in the park, taking the air in a sedan chair, but in his later years he travelled in a closed carriage, which no-one was allowed to approach for fear of an attack. He was seen walking in the park in deep conversation with Colonels Fleetwood and Desborough on the day before Parliament formally asked him to take the Crown.

Charles II loved this park; he planned and laid it out with Le Notre, walked with his dogs, and fed the wild-fowl and the birds in cages hung from trees on the south side which were cared for by one Edmund Storey. The road on that side is today called Birdcage Walk, and one of the entrances is Storey's Gate. The king merged several small ponds into a canal, with a duck decoy; there are accounts surviving relating to this work:

Charles Rex – the works and services comprised in this account were done by our direction, 30 May 1671.

To Edward Dudley, Robert Beard and others – for 670 loads of gravel, for ye raising of the Longe Walk, and several causey-ways to St James's Park, in the year 1663 at the rate of twelve pence a load = £33.10s.

To Edward Maybanke & Thomas Green – for 1,023 loads of gravel at eight pence the load = £34.2s.

To severall persons for carrying rubbish and gravell into the said Parke and spreading it – ten pounds fifteen shillings.

To Philip Moore, Gardener – for directing the levelling of the ground of the pond by the Horse-ground; and the ground by the Canall side, fifteen pounds, fifteen shillings.

To Edward Maybanke and Thomas Green for digging the Decoy, carrying out the earth, levelling the ground about the said Decoy, one hundred and twenty eight pounds, two shillings and elevenpence halfpenny.

To Edward Storey – for wyer and other things used about the Decoy, and to 100 baskets for the ducks – eight pounds nine shillings.

To Oliver Honey for paving the feeding-place for the ducks and breaking the ground – one pound, ten shillings.

To Sir George Waterman – for severall netts for the Decoy – fifteen pounds, three shillings.

To James Rimes – for plants, setts and four hundred bolts of reeds for the use of the Decoy – fifteen pounds, eleven shillings and eight pence.

To Edmund Storey – for money paid to sundry workmen – for setting the reeds and polles round the Decoy, and wyering it – nine pounds, ten shillings.

To Sydrack Hilcus, for ye contriving of the Decoy in St James's Park – thirty pounds.

For looking to the plantacion, and pruning the trees in St James's Parke – seventy three pounds and seven pence.

73. Portrait of Charles I, by Daniel Mytens, 1631.

74. Portrait of Oliver Cromwell, by Robert Walker, c.1649.

75. Storey's Gate in 1820.

76. Rosamund's Pond, pre-1770.

For oatmeal, tares, hemp-seed and other corn for the birds and the fowls from September 1660 to 24 June 1670 – two hundred and forty six pounds, eighteen shillings.
To William Thawsell for fish for the cormorant – 12 March 1661 – one pound, thirteen shillings.
To John Scott for Carpenter's worke done in wharfing, and to making bridges, and for boards used about the Decoy, and other work – forty five pounds, fifteen shillings and fourpence.

Charles obviously enjoyed supervising this work, and 160 years later the Prince Regent, with Nash as his architect, took as much pleasure in creating the lake in its present state.

A rather gloomy pond at the western end remained after Charles's work, and was known as Rosamund's Pond. A 'place for lovers meeting', Jesse said in 1840. 'The romantic appearance, overshadowing trees, the view of the venerable Abbey made it a favourite resort of the contemplative, attracting a greater number of suicides, especially female, than any other place in London'. Wycherley and Congreve both used it as a setting for plays. It was filled in during 1770.

At the end of the canal was Duck Island. Walpole joked in a letter that 'My Lord Pomfret is made Ranger of the Park, and in consequence, my Lady is Queen of Duck Island'. The animals with which the king stocked the park were noted by John Evelyn in his diary on 9 February 1665:

The Park was at this time stored with numerous flocks of severall sorts of ordinary and extraordinary wildfowle, breeding about the Decoy, which, for being neere so great a citty and among such a concourse of souldiers, guards and people, is very diverting. There were also deere of several countries, white, spotted like Leopards; Antelope, and Elk, Red Deere, Roebucks, Stagg's, Guinea Goates, Arabian Sheepe, etc. Withy-pots, or nests for the wild fowle to lay in, a little above the surface of the water was very pretty. I examined the throat of a pelican. Also, two balearian cranes, one of which having had its leg broken and cut off above the knee – it had a wooden leg and thigh with a joint so accurately made, that the poor creature could walk with it. It was made by a soldier.

The *London Gazette* of 30 October 1690 reported on the promised prosecution of any poachers of the wild life in the park: 'And whosoever shall give information to John Webb, living in St James's Palace (the Keeper), shall have a gratuity for every gun, nett, dog or any engine, that shall be seized and taken from any such offender'.

Charles II was fond of all animals. It was discovered in 1786, 100 years after his death, that a charge was still made at the King's Mews, every year, for hemp-seed. 'It was allowed that none was used, but the charge had been regularly made since the reign of Charles II, and it was recollected that this good natured Monarch was as fond of his ducks as his dogs and took pleasure in feeding those on the canal. It was concluded this expense began in his time, continued to be charged for regularly, though none was used or provided'. Further evidence of this side of the 'Merry Monarch's' nature comes from an advertisement in the *London Gazette*:

Lost, four or five days since, in St James's Park, a dogg of his Majesty's, full of blew spots, with a white cross on his forehead and about the bigness of a tumbler. The persons who have found or have taken up the said dogg are to give notice thereof to the Porter of the Palace.

The park, however, was always a centre of human, as well as animal, activity. The winter of 1662 was cold. John Evelyn wrote on 1 December of 'Having seen the strange and wonderful dexterity of the sliders in the new canal in St James's Park, performed by divers gentlemen and others with skeets, after the manner of the Hollander, with what swiftness they pass!'. And Samuel Pepys wrote in his journal on 15 December 1662: 'To the Duke – and followed him into the Park, where, although the ice was broken, he would go and slide on his skates, which I did not like, but he slides very well'. Two years later, in the summer, Pepys wrote on 10 August 1664: 'Lords Castlehaven and Arran running down and killing a stout buck, for a wager, before the King'. Skating was still a novelty 47 years later. Jonathan Swift commented in a letter to Stella in January 1711 that it was 'Delicate walking weather, the canal and Rosamund's Pond full of rabble, sliding – with skates, if you know what that means'.

During the State Visit in 1814 of the Allied Sovereigns, a Chinese bridge with a seven-storey pagoda was built over the lake, and during the firework display it caught fire. There were revellers in boats and the trees were hung with Chinese lanterns. It

77. Feeding the ducks in St James's Park, c. 1890.

78. The Pagoda fire, 1814.

79. The Milk Fair in St James's Park.

was one of those fantastic evenings at which London excels, despite the destruction of the pagoda. The first permanent lighting of the main paths was provided by gas in 1822.

Milk was sold in St James's Park as late as the 1840s: 'the principal sale of milk from the cow is in St James's Park. The once fashionable drink known as sillabub – the milk being drawn warm from the cow's udder upon a portion of wine, sugar, spices, etc – is now unknown. As the sellers of milk in the park are merely the servants of cow-keepers, and attend to the sale as part of their business, no notice is required. They obtain leave from the Home Secretary to ply their trade. There are eight stands in summer, but in winter, only four'.

In February 1905 Mr. E. W. Braybrook wrote a letter to *The Times*, quite distressed at finding no cows. 'Sixty years ago, it was one of the delights of my youth; to city boys, our only chance of seeing a cow; the only remaining evidence of the famous Spring Gardens. I hope the authorities will restore the cows, to remove them was a tyrannous action'. It is interesting that Elizabeth Cromwell, wife of the Protector, kept a cow in the park in 1656.

Is there a ghost in St James's Park? In January 1804 the figure of a headless woman was seen to glide across the Park to the canal where it vanished into thin air, or slipped into the water. It was recalled that about 1784 a sergeant of the guard had murdered his wife by cutting off her head, and had thrown the body into the canal. Officers of the Coldstream Guards took statements from sentries, claiming that they had seen the ghost, but descriptions varied so wildly that the affair was dropped and a general assumption that the men were drunk.

Green Park

Green Park is bounded by Piccadilly on the north, Constitution Hill on the south, and Queen's Walk (which runs from Piccadilly to the Mall, under the windows of Bridgewater House and Lancaster House) on the east. It is a triangle of lush grass and trees. There are no flower beds, only natural woodland, except for the paths. Charles II first enclosed it, but with none of the planning that went into St James's Park. For Henry VIII, of course, it had just been part of his hunting preserve. The River Tyburn ran across the park, creating a pool in the hollow, but is now trapped underground. Constitution Hill used to be roughly the centre of the park, but when George III moved into Buckingham Palace he took about a third of the park to enlarge the Palace Garden, the wall of which runs the length of this street.

Three attempts were made on Constitution Hill to assassinate Queen Victoria. Firstly on 10 June 1840 a man named Oxford fired at her; then on 30 May 1842 a man named Francis did likewise; and finally on 19 May 1849 the papers reported 'an idiot named Hamilton'. On 29 June 1850 Sir Robert Peel was thrown from his horse here and died three days later.

This was always a bad area for violence. For example, a report in the *St James's Chronicle* of 2 November 1769 stated that 'a gang of desperate villains infest the Green Park, that no person can pass there of an evening'. Once, when King George I was dismounting near Stable Yard, one Margaret Nicholson struck at him with a knife, which slipped harmlessly between his waistcoat and great-coat. Again, on 17 August 1791, George III was riding in the park when a man of gentle appearance, dressed in black, stuck a piece of paper in the railings and shot himself.

Despite this, by 1785 Queen's Walk, laid down for Queen Caroline in 1730, had become the setting for a fashionable promenade, so that seats in windows and balconies overlooking it were in demand: a Mr. Rigby paid £400 for such a seat!

This park was also a favourite setting for duels. Fielding fought Sir Henry Colt here, over some imagined favour from Charles II's mistress, the Duchess of Cleveland. They chose to hold the duel under her very windows! Poulteney and Lord Hervey also – Hervey had attacked Poulteney in a pamphlet, and Poulteney replied with an acrimonious description of Hervey as 'the gayest of the gay'. So – of course – a duel! Poulteney had the best of the fight until his foot slipped on the wet grass. Their seconds rushed in to stop the fight, and Poulteney embraced Hervey, promising never to abuse him again.

One contemporary writer, Peter Underwood, claims that one particular tree – he does not say which one – seems to repel people. 'No one picnics under it, no children play near. Sounds of a man's voice that ceases as soon as you are aware of it, a low cunning laugh and a moaning sound of someone in despair'. He adds 'the tree is a favourite one for suicides'.

Underwood does not mention the ghost which is reputed to appear at the little gate leading from Queen's Walk into Stable Yard, by Lancaster House. This alley is called Milkmaid's Passage, or Dairymaid's Walk, because the cows were driven

80. (*above left*) Portrait of Queen Victoria, by Lady
Julia Abercromby, after Heinrich von Angeli, 1883.

81. (*above*) Portrait of George I, studio of Sir Godfrey
Kneller.

82. (*left*) Portrait of George III, studio of Allan
Ramsay, *c.*1767.

83. Milkmaid's Passage, where cows were driven in to Stable Yard from Green Park to be milked.

through here from the park to the Palace stable yard for milking. Inspector Mabon of the Metropolitan Police has stated that 'Several times we were called to St James's by guards on duty, someone was rattling the gate and calling "let me in, let me in". The next time it happened one police car was stationed at the end of Queen's Walk in Piccadilly, another at the bottom of The Mall, and officers on foot moved across the Park to the gate, and again – no one! A Park Keeper has since told me this rattling and calling out has been heard many times'. The author has walked in the park at different times of day and night, hovered hopefully and silently in Milkmaid's Passage, and left in disappointment.

Close to the intersection, where six paths converge with a gas lamp in the centre, is a large manhole cover under which can be heard the old River Tyburn storming along underground.

84. Lancaster House in 1825.

85. The Grand Staircase in Lancaster House, 1830.

Lancaster House

There are three great houses within the complex of buildings collectively known as St James's Palace, and one which is just outside. On the ground where Lancaster House now stands, prior to 1685 stood a laundry, about 200 feet square, a decent distance from the royal apartments. In that year a lease of the site was granted by James II to Lady Oglethorpe for 31 years, at an annual rent of 10s., and she built Harrington House thereon. It has been suggested that the lady was given such a favourable site, at such a low rent, because she was intimately concerned in the so-called 'Warming-pan Plot' – that is, that James II's son was born dead, or non-existent, and that Lady Oglethorpe's baby, newly-born himself, was substituted in a warming-pan and grew up to become the 'Old Pretender'.

Six years later the lease was granted to Lord Lexington for 99 years. It was then acquired by Lord Godolphin, who enlarged the house where his family were to live for over 100 years. He was the third member of what was known as the 'Trinity' – the Duke of Marlborough dominated the successful army, his Duchess dominated Queen Anne, and Godolphin was the political power. That dominance was broken in 1710; Anne died in 1714, and by 1737 George II had built on this spot a small building for Queen Caroline to house her library, close to the house. This building eventually became a lumber-room.

On 26 August 1807 the Duke of York, second son of George III, was given a lease of 98 years, and for a time the library reverted to its former purpose, as in 1815 the Duke brought his books there from the Horseguards for storage. The site was then levelled and the present building begun by Wyatt in 1825. The Duke had intended to make this his permanent London home, but he died in 1827.

The house was bought by the Marquis of Stafford, who had lent the Duke the money to build in the first place. He added the upper storey.

So the house has had five names – Harrington, Godolphin, York, Stafford, and now Lancaster, as it has been known since 1912, when Lord Leverhulme bought and presented it to the nation; it is now used for international conferences and Government hospitality. (Do not be confused by the name 'York'. The part of the Palace *now* known as York House is that older range, lying between Cleveland Row and Ambassador's Court. Lancaster House was only 'York' for the short period of the Duke's ownership.)

It is, doubtless, one of the most magnificent buildings in London. It was described, in 1850, as follows:

> The interior is by Barry, who also added the upper storey. The grandest feature is the hall and staircase, opening through all the storeys with a lantern filled with engraved glass and supported by eighteen palm trees; the whole is a square of eighty feet, rising in the centre to 120 feet. The floor, red and white marble; when lighted by candelabra, the effect is truly gorgeous.

Chancellor said in 1908 (when it was still Stafford House, although Stafford himself had become the Duke of Sutherland), 'Stafford is the largest, within the most gorgeous, without the most unostentatious of London's private Palaces'. Queen Victoria once said to the Duke of Sutherland: 'I have come from my house to your Palace'.

86. A guard outside Clarence House in 1986.

Clarence House

This house was built by Nash in 1825 for the Duke of Clarence, who became William IV. It is now the London residence of Queen Elizabeth, the Queen Mother. On the death of William IV the young Princess Victoria became Queen, at the age of 18 years. She had always lived under the complete domination of her mother, the Duchess of Kent. As Queen she insisted upon a separate residence, and the Duchess moved into Clarence House.

In 1866 the house was allotted to the Queen's second son, Prince Albert; and during alterations we are informed that very old foundations were uncovered, stretching out far into the garden, thought to be the remains of old Stafford House. This must have been under Stable Yard Road, as the garden which lies between Clarence House and the wall which lines the Mall is believed to be substantially as it was in Charles I's reign.

The top storey was added in 1873/4, a new wing was added, and the old portico, at that time facing Lancaster House, was removed, and a new entrance made facing the Mall and St James's Park. Clarence

87.   Portrait of William IV, by M. A. Shee.

House holds many happy memories for the Queen and Prince Philip; in the days before her accession they lived here when in London.

One of the author's delights, on the Queen Mother's birthday, is to hear the Guards' Band play 'Happy Birthday to You' as they march to Buckingham Palace for the Changing of the Guard. Her Majesty, enchanting as always, then comes out of the house to greet the crowds of people who have gathered to sing their good wishes.

88. Portrait of John Churchill, 1st Duke of Marlborough, attributed to J. Closterman after J. Riley.

89. Portrait of Sarah Churchill, Duchess of Marlborough, after Sir Godfrey Kneller, c.1700.

Marlborough House

In the reign of Charles II, on the ground now occupied by this house and the Queen's Chapel, stood the Friary, part of the establishment of Queen Catherine. Samuel Pepys's diary records that on 16 January 1667, when he was shown round by the Queen's Almoner, Cardinal Howard, he 'saw the Dortoire, and the cells of the priests, and we went into one, a very pretty little room, very clean, hung with pictures and set with books. The Priest was in his cell with his hair-clothes next to his skin, bare-legged with a sandall only on, and his little bed without sheets, and no feather-bed, and yet, I thought, comfortable enough'.

Nearby was part of the Palace garden where Charles I had planted an acorn from the Boscobel oak in which he had hidden to evade capture from Cromwell's men; this grew into a flourishing tree. This house was built by Wren in 1709 for the victorious soldier, the Duke of Marlborough, and his lovely tempestuous Duchess, Sarah, who asked Queen Anne for a long lease of Crown Land adjoining the Palace on the east, to build their London home. Sarah laid the foundation stone on 24 May 1709. People were very angry because Charles' oak tree was wantonly torn down and destroyed.

It is hard to discern Wren's work in the building today: the third and fourth floors are much later additions, the interior completely altered.

In 1722 the Duke died, but old Sarah lived on in this house, delighting to disparage 'her neighbour George', when George I came to the throne. The Marlborough family held the lease until 1817.

The Duchess had other neighbours apart from the king; completely accustomed to having her own way, by these people she was caused much angry frustration. The *Daily Journal* of 6 January 1733 reported that 'Yesterday, her Grace the Dowager Duchess of Marlborough, viewed several old houses in the Friery of St James's, being about to purchase them in order to be pulled down, making the entrance to her house more spacious. The Duchess intended to improve the entrance to the courtyard – an archway was opened in the wall, but had to be blocked up; her Grace was frustrated by Sir Robert Walpole who, to annoy her, bought the requisite houses in Pall Mall'.

Others of lesser rank than Sir Robert also defied her: various houses in Pall Mall had encroached eight feet beyond the lease, and the people who lived there 'committed many trespasses which made things uneasy and disagreeable', and the Duchess's heaviest cross was 'the corner house in the passage, a miserable, mean and rotten house'. She persuaded the Board of Green Cloth, which licensed alehouses, to withdraw its licence 'it being a great nuisance, they putting out all manner of nastiness in the way, I must go to my house'. The last of the old buildings between Marlborough House and St James's Palace was removed by Vardy in 1748.

Edward and Alexandra, Prince and Princess of Wales, moved into this house in May 1863. The Prince Consort had died in 1861; Queen Victoria had become an inconsolable recluse, and London revolved around Edward and Alexandra. When the hall paper was stripped, old paintings of Marlborough's battles were revealed on the walls. The house was filled with people, parties, life. G. & W. Fisher, in their book *Bertie and Alex*, write:

90. (*above*) Hackney cab rank at Marlborough House Gate, *c.*1902.

91. (*below*) Marlborough House entrance, 1986.

In the house and vast echoing basement with its furnace, china store, linen room, housekeeper's store, silver pantry, and wine cellar, Bertie and Alex had 85 servants at their beck and call. Three or four men did nothing else but clean silver, two more attended to more than 300 bowls of flowers. Whilst the princess still slept, the Prince of Wales, after a brisk early morning stroll in the Park, would breakfast in his walnut panelled sitting room, looking out onto the Clubs of Pall Mall, the first skirl of the bagpipes reaching him from the piper in the garden.

In July 1874 the Prince and Princess of· Wales held an enormously extravagant fancy dress ball for 1,400 guests. The prince dressed as Charles I, Alexandra as a Venetian princess. On the Diamond Jubilee of Queen Victoria the outside of Marlborough House was decorated with the Queen's VR cipher, and the Prince of Wales feathers. Electric light was used, though the lamps short circuited when the princess pressed the button to illuminate them'.

An amusing comment on the life of the staff in the 19th century comes from R. Kerr, *The Gentleman's House* (1865):

The kitchen of Marlborough House and the Dining Room also, are at ground level. But to carry the dinner across the entrance court and in at the front door would never do. To carry it round by the garden and in at the saloon door would never do. We might contrive a third route – along the colonnade, in at the library window, and through the rooms and corridors – but this is still a jest. The actual route was; downstairs to the basement, through the corridors, dark as palladian basements generally were – upstairs again, by any of the three staircases, and on to the Dining Room. Why all this inconvenience? It would seem the idea in the architect's mind was that the kitchen would make a good wing – an obtrusive and sham two-storey house, with a door onto the courtyard. So, unhappy footmen, for a hundred years or so, must stumble upstairs and downstairs with the soup tureens and barons of beef!

92.   Bridgewater House in 1983, fronting on to Green Park.

Bridgewater House

This is the fourth house, and the one not strictly 'Palace'; however, not only its close proximity but also its close ties with the King's mistress give excellent qualification for its inclusion. In the reign of Charles I the Earl of Berkshire built a mansion on this site, with gardens to the south towards Lancaster House, and to the east along Cleveland Row, when the garden wall faced the Palace, as far as St James's Street. He called it Berkshire House, and it is shown on Faithorne's Map of 1658. Lord Clarendon stayed here and was visited by Samuel Pepys and John Evelyn.

On 8 May 1668 Charles II bought the house as a residence for his lovely Barbara. She was the wife of Roger Palmer, an 'accommodating gentleman'. The king created him Earl of Castlemaine in 1661 in order that Barbara should become Lady Castlemaine. He lived here for almost a year and then discreetly left the field to the king. Was he a rogue, a complacent, well rewarded cuckold, or a desperately unhappy man? History is silent. By 1670 Lady Castlemaine was created Duchess of Cleveland, and the house became Cleveland House.

Although, as we have already seen (p. 55), Barbara sold some of her grounds in order to pay off her debts, on her death in 1709 the house went to her son, the Duke of Cleveland, who lived happily in it until his death in 1730.

The house was then bought by the first Duke of Bridgewater, and the name changed for the last time. The third Duke enlarged it in 1795; but it was sold in 1833 to Lord Ellesmere, who completely rebuilt it in 1849 to a design by Barry, who, incidentally, wanted to drive Pall Mall straight through Cleveland Row to Green Park, suggesting that the Marble Arch be placed between Lancaster and Bridgewater Houses!

93.   View of St James's Palace and Pall Mall in 1753.

94.   Cabs outside St James's Palace.

The History of St James's Palace

Earlier, we discovered the origins of the Palace 900 years ago, as a tiny, isolated hospital. Since that time the Palace has been altered, burned, and rebuilt, many times. The Great Gatehouse, Clock Tower and turrets are still entirely Tudor as, of course, are the State Rooms. As the centuries went by, generations of builders have worked on it, but these areas have always retained their Tudor characters, often with original salvaged material.

The original boundaries and courtyards remain almost unchanged. Ambassador's Court was once divided into two tiny courtyards by a building running north to south, and Friary Court was formerly an enclosed quadrangle lying between the east and west wings of the royal private apartments.

However, the Palace was once much larger: a fire in the early 19th century destroyed an entire wing which ran west to east along the Mall. Many documents were lost, breaking the continuity of the records.

Structural change took place for many reasons, sometimes to create a more impressive building, as Olwen Hedley explains in her book *Royal Palaces*:

> When Henry VIII built it, a pretty coherence linked the turretted gatehouse on the north, with the Royal wings facing the Park. The original precision had been lost when Henry Flitcroft made his plan in 1729. Christopher Wren had carried the south front westward with the addition for James II of the Great-Drawing Room and the king's politically suspect Great Council Chamber; and more royal apartments far beyond the confines of the present Palace, had been built on the east and the north.

However, each royal occupant adapted the building to his own needs, thus when James I gave St James's Palace to his son, Prince Henry, in 1604, some alterations were felt to be necessary:

> Whereas St James's Howse is appoynted by His Majesty for the prince to lye at, unto the which there is neither barn nor stable belonginge, the which wante, of necessite must be supplyed. These are, therefore, to pray you to draw a warrant unto the Lord High Treasurer to gyve this direction unto the Office of His Majesty's Works for the buildinge of such conveniente stablinge and barne rooms as shall there be founde needful for the prince's service. – Whitehall, the 14 July, 1604; your lovinge friend, E Worcester.
> To the Right Worshipful Sir Thomas Lake, Clerk of His Majesty's Signett

Here, therefore, is an example of building work undertaken for practical reasons. The letter also reveals the date of the stables, which are on the north side of Stable Yard, facing Lancaster House and which were carefully restored in 1980.

The story of the Palace is best told chronologically under monarchs: but one part of it deserves special attention.

95. & 96.   Two views of St James's
Palace gatehouse in about 1840.

97. Roofline of St James's Palace, showing the clock tower on the Great Gates.

98. Friary Court.

99. View of Colour Court from above, with the Great Gate turret to the left and Marlborough House in the background.

100. The old stable arches before renovation.

101. (*left*) The stable arches after renovation in 1984.

102. (*above*) Outside the Stable Yard Gate, with Lancaster House on the left and Clarence House on the right.

THE CHAPEL ROYAL

This is almost certainly on the foundations of the consecrated site of the Leper Hospital Chapel of 1100; the Norman masonry discovered during building alterations in 1838 is a very strong pointer to this being the case. It lies between Colour Court and Ambassador's Court. It must not be confused with the later Queen's Chapel near Marlborough House, which is of the mid-17th century, built for Charles I's queen, Henrietta Maria.

In 1834, during alterations, panels were discovered, inscribed *Stet Dieux Felix Henricus Rex VIII-HA Vivat Rex 1540. Dieu et mon droit.* Thos initials, HA, found elsewhere in the Palace, are popularly believed to mean Henry and Anne Boleyn, but with that date of 1540 it must be Anne of Cleves, whom Henry did not love!

The Chapel Royal today is substantially the same building as when John Evelyn watched Charles I at prayer. You can see the date '1540' in several places on the Holbein ceiling. It is a tiny building holding only 160 worshippers. Charles had

103. The Chapel Royal: an engraving by Radclyffe.

104. Painting of Lady Mary Wortley Montagu and her son, attributed to J. B. Vanmour.

renewed and repaired the Chapel to make it fit for divine service, after it had seen use as a guardroom; it was here that the King attended his last service, before he walked across the park to the scaffold.

This was the fashionable place to be seen in during the 18th century. Lady Mary Wortley Montagu wrote to her daughter, Lady Bute: 'I must confess I remember to have dressed for St James's Chapel with the same thought your daughters will have for the Opera'. In the early 17th century, however, it would seem that visitors to the Chapel were of a ruder kind. James I felt it necessary to order that 'Noe man whatsoever to presume to wayte upon us to the Chappel in bootes and spurs. The Porter to repell all that presume to bring with them any pistolls, daggers, cudgells or other unfit weapons'.

George III was a most regular worshipper. Fanny Burney recorded an amusing vignette in her journal: 'the Queen and other members of the Royal family, dropping off to sleep one by one during the sermon, leaving the king, the Parson and the Equerry to sit it out together'.

Each year the Epiphany offering of gold, frankincense and myrrh is made here on behalf of the Queen.

HENRY VIII

Henry VIII built this Palace in 1532, his 'Mannor House' for Anne Boleyn. For an early description of the building, we go forward a little in time to Queen Elizabeth's Surveyor, Norden, in 1598. He had just described Westminster Hall, and continued:

> not far from this glorious Hall, another house descryeth itself, of a quadrate form, erected in bricke; the exterior shape whereof, though it appears without any sumptuous devyces, yet is the spot very princelye. It standeth from other buildings about two furlongs, saving a farmehouse opposite of its North Gate. On the east, London offereth itself in view; in the South, the stateley buyldings of Westminster; with the pleasant Park and the delights thereof. On the north, the green feeldes. The situation is pleasant, indued with a good ayre, and pleasant prospects.

Mr. Stubbs of Kingston-upon-Thames supplied Samwelle bricks at 2s. 8d. per thousand; Caen stone came from Normandy; there was much gold leaf, for the initials HA, among other things, which are still to be seen. It took 211 workmen, with six clerks as foremen (five of whom were paid 6d. a day with the 'gaffer' receiving 8d.) to raise the Hunting Lodge, with Thomas Cromwell supervising the building, possibly to a design by the artist Holbein.

It was centred on Friary Court, with Henry's rooms on the west side and Anne's on the east. Here they lived and loved among the brilliance of a Tudor court, with enormous meals, music, dancing, and intrigues in every corner; and plenty of hunting, for all the present parks and well beyond were preserves for the King's pleasure. Barely three years later Anne had lost his love and her head, and the house was hardly used during the rest of Henry's reign.

Whilst he was in residence, however, the Palace was under the jurisdiction of the 'Board of Green Cloth', so called from the table at which the officers sit. The jurisdiction of the Board extended over the 'Verge of Court', or 12 miles round the residence of the sovereign. To the Board belonged the sole right of arrest within the limits of the Palace. Here is an example of the court in session, on 10 June 1541:

> Sir Edmund Knevet was arraigned before the Officers of the Green Cloth for striking Master Cleer within the king's house; being found guilty, he had judgement to lose his right hand, and forfeit his lands and goods. He desired only, that if the king would spare his right hand and take the left, he may yet live to give the king good service: when the king was informed, he granted him to lose neither hand, and pardoned him also of his house and goods.

The Board was eventually abolished in 1849, but in its day it supervised all aspects of the royal household, including the household accounts. The warrant book of Board of Green Cloth for 12 June 1561 tells us that 'Order was this day given that the Maids of Honour should have Cherry Tarts instead of Gooseberry Tarts, it being observed that cherries are at three pence per pound'. How one would love to think that the farm opposite the gate, where Rothman's shop is today, supplied those cherries and gooseberries.

EDWARD VI

There is very little record of Henry's sickly young son, Edward VI, using the Palace, though he did bring his father's sixth and last wife, Catherine Parr, here for short periods. Still a child, the kingdom was ruled by regents; he died tragically early and Mary I became Queen in 1555.

MARY

Mary loved St James's Palace, using it as her private residence, and keeping Whitehall for official functions. Her bitter persecution of the Protestants, and her decision to marry Philip of Spain, caused Thomas Wyatt and his rebellious Men of Kent to march on London. She died of typhoid fever at St James's, a lonely and embittered woman, in 1558. These two short reigns were followed by the 45 glorious years of Elizabeth I – that true Tudor daughter of Henry VIII and Anne Boleyn's passionate and stormy love.

ELIZABETH I

Elizabeth knew St James's from childhood visits; as Queen she did not make it her permanent home for she never stayed long in any one place. 'Progresses' were constant, involving long journeys to see and to be seen by the people.

In July 1588 Elizabeth moved into St James's to wait for the message which would tell of victory or defeat in the battle with the Spanish Armada. Two special forces were detailed, one to guard the Queen at the Palace, one to await the invaders at Tilbury in case the battle was lost.

Elizabeth died in 1603, and with her ended the Tudor dynasty.

JAMES I

James, the son of Mary Queen of Scots and the ill-fated Darnley, now came to the throne. He moved into the Palace of Whitehall, and rarely visited St James's, which he gave as an official residence to his son, Henry, Prince of Wales. James did, however, appoint William Shakespeare to be Groom of the Chamber in attendance to the Constable of Castile, whilst the latter was on a visit to this country and accommodated at St James's Palace. Shakespeare was given a fee of £14 8s. for 18 days; the 'post' was almost certainly a means of making the playwright a handsome gift.

105. Portrait of James I, by Daniel Mytens, c.1621.

106. Portrait of Henry, Prince of Wales, by R. Peake, c.1610.

James also brought Lord Lumley's extensive library to be housed here, most surely to the great pleasure of Prince Henry, a scholar with several languages, a wit, an all-round sportsman and a soldier.

Prince Henry held sumptuous court here. He was most concerned with etiquette: his Grooms of the Chamber were reminded 'not to come into the Prince's Presence with their doublets unbuttoned, or hose untied'.

He held tournaments at which he challenged allcomers to fight, and was fond of hosting great feasts at night in St James's. Tragically, Henry died here of typhoid fever on 6 November 1612: 'the people making great moan at the Gate'. Had he not died at this time, English history might have taken a different course, for his death meant that his younger brother became Charles I in 1625. These two brothers were so different in character, yet both of them died tragically, and St James's Palace was the final home for them both.

CHARLES I

107. Portrait of John Donne, after Isaac Oliver.

James I died on 27 March 1625. Upon his accession, Charles came to St James's, remained in complete seclusion for a week, and on Sunday 3 April requested that a sermon be preached at Evensong in the Chapel Royal by John Donne. The King left his private apartment, 'dined in the Privy Chamber, being dressed in a plain black cloak to the ancles', and afterwards attended the service.

In the same year Charles married the French princess, Henrietta Maria, who loved St James's Palace. Her favourite architect, Inigo Jones, already planning a private chapel for the Queen, enlarged the Palace also. The royal couple's eldest children, Charles and James, were both born here. For the first child, apartments were made ready on the south front (facing the Mall), and a bed of green satin, embroidered by Charles Gentile at a cost of £670, was set up. For the second child, the Queen chose a bed of tawny velvet, although the unfortunate Gentile still had not received payment for the green one!

The charming Queen's Chapel was built for Queen Henrietta Maria's private use as she was a Catholic. You can see it today by the side of Marlborough House: in the 17th century it was not divided from the Palace by a busy road.

When the Queen's mother, Maria de Medici, visited her daughter with great ceremony in 1638, we learn that the Palace had grown to a considerable size. The French nobleman, the Sieur de la Serre, said that the Quartermaster was able to reserve 50 apartments for the French Queen and her household, and spoke lyrically of their rich furnishings. Charles had filled St James's with many art treasures.

With the outbreak of the Civil War in 1642, St James's was left abandoned and empty. When the Parliamentarians captured Charles's youngest children, Elizabeth, Henry and Henrietta, they were imprisoned in the Palace. Lady Dalkeith managed to smuggle Henrietta away to Holland – herself disguised as a hunch-back and Henrietta as a boy, protesting loudly and volubly that she was a Stuart princess.

James was captured at the Battle of Edgehill, and also brought back to St James's and imprisonment, guarded by Cromwell's men: but he also escaped, by playing a regular game of 'hide and seek' with his captors in the garden. Day after day, he gradually extended his absence, and found more difficult hiding places; then, finally, on the arranged day he shut up his dog, who might have followed him, obtained the key of the garden gate from the gardener, and slipped into St James's Park, where friends were waiting in a coach with a disguise for him. By the time his guards had discovered that the prince was not just hiding, and reported his escape to the Parliamentarian commander, General Fairfax, at Whitehall, James had gone down-river to Gravesend, and taken ship for the Continent.

Charles I was captured and brought here on 9 January 1649 to become a prisoner in his own Palace. His eldest son, Charles, was still in hiding. Although James and Henrietta had escaped, Elizabeth and Henry were still here, under guard. In those few days before his trial in Westminster Hall, initially, the King was treated with every courtesy, his meals served with ceremony and in privacy. Later, meals were brought in by the guards, and he was constantly interrupted and scorned.

He was sentenced to death on 27 January 1649. Oliver Cromwell was one of the judges, and also one of the signatories to the death warrant. On his return to St James's Palace, the King sent for a casket of jewels, trifles to give his children, when they came to him to say their farewells. Afterwards, the Princess Elizabeth, aged 13, said: 'He wished me not to grieve, it would be a gracious death to die'.

To his youngest son, Henry, Duke of Gloucester, he said 'Sweetheart, now they will cut off they father's head; mark child, what I say, they will cut off my head and perhaps make thee a king. But mark what I say, you must *not* be a king, so long as your brothers, Charles and James, do live; for they will cut off your brothers' heads when they can catch them, and cut off thy head, too, at the last, and therefore I charge thee, do not be made a king by them'. The sobbing boy said 'I will be torn in pieces first'.

This is John Buchan's description of the day of the execution:

It was grey and very cold, there were ice floes in the Thames. Charles rose a little after 5.00 a.m. and bade Thomas Herbert dress him carefully, giving him an extra shirt. 'By reason, the season is so sharp that it will probably make me shake, which some will imagine comes from fear. I will have no such imputation. I fear not death, death is not terrible to me. I bless God, I am prepared'.
He put on the George, and the Garter Riband. Bishop Juxon arrived to pray with him. Then Colonel Hacker bade him get ready to go to Whitehall. In the bitter morning, the King left St James's Palace for the last time, attended by Juxon, Colonel Tomlinson and the guards. The King walked across the Park, briskly, as was his custom.

The body was brought back to St James's; and he lay there for a week. At one time, legend has it, a silent figure in a cloak was seen standing by the bier in silence for a long time and then left, muttering 'Dreadful necessity'. It was believed to have been Oliver Cromwell. On Friday 9 February the body was carried from here. The bier was covered in a black velvet pall, which became covered in snow before it arrived at Windsor Castle to be placed in the same vault as Henry VIII and Jane Seymour. Henrietta Maria was told of her husband's death by Henry Jermyn.

Oliver Cromwell continued to use St James's Palace, as an army barracks. Various Royalists, including the Duke of Hamilton, the Earl of Norwich and Sir John Owen, were imprisoned here before their trials.

Cromwell began to sell the lovely art treasures with which Charles had filled the Palace: works by Raphael, Holbein, Titian, Da Vinci, Corregio, Carravagio,

Tintoretto, Rubens, Van Dyck: the monarchs of France, Sweden and Spain were among the buyers. The famous Van Dyck triptych of Charles was not among these; it had been sent to Bellini in Italy, as an aid to a sculpture he was doing of Charles, and is now at Windsor; the superb Raphael Cartoons, which Charles had bought on Rubens' advice, also escaped. These pictures still form part of the royal collection.

The Library was still fairly intact at the Restoration of the Monarchy, but in an appalling condition. Even nine years before, the Librarian was complaining that 'books and manuscripts will be utterly ruined as they lie upon the floor in confused heaps; ... not only dust and rain, but rats can easily get to them'. This library was originally formed by Prince Edward, the short-lived son of Henry VIII, with a collection made by John Leland at the dissolution of the monasteries. Leland presented them to Edward, who appointed Bartholomew Trahon, the first Keeper, at twenty shillings a year. This collection was subsequently dispersed, but James I refounded the Library and appointed Isaac Casaubon as Librarian. Many years later, in 1757, the entire collection was presented to the British Museum by George II.

CHARLES II

On the night Oliver Cromwell died in 1658 a violent storm raged over the country and many of the trees in St James's Park were uprooted. There followed some months of unrest and uncertainty, as many were unwilling to accept Cromwell's son as ruler. St James's Palace, still an army barracks, became the centre of army resistance where General Monck planned the Restoration of the Monarchy. After prolonged negotiations, Charles II finally returned to his kingdom, arriving in London on 25 May 1660 amid scenes of the wildest rejoicing.

St James's now came into its own, the background for scenes of Stuart splendour, and for the many love affairs of the King and his brother, James, Duke of York. St James's Palace was repaired and refurnished; many of the art treasures sold by Cromwell were returned by the buyers; the old rooms glowed with candlelight, laughter and music. The new monarch was besieged by petitions, quite a number of which related to positions at court. John Rose asked for reinstatement as Keeper and Gardener of the Park – was he the gardener who gave James the key to escape? Henry de Puy asked to be 'Master of the Pall Mall'. Thomas Ross requested payment of all the money he had spent recovering much of the Library from the buyers, and cataloguing it – he was given £200 a year.

108. St James's Palace and parks, after Hollar 1660, published in 1809.

The park was laid out, the ubiquitous Henry Jermyn was building upon those 'green feeldes' of St James's. There must have been a constant swirl of movement from the Palace, about the streets and the houses, the inns and shops.

The Palace (and many nearby houses) became the setting for the King's pursuit of his mistresses. There were 12 mistresses of whose names we may be sure; there were, most certainly, more. Of Lucy Walters, we know very little: they met during his exile and she bore him the ill-fated Duke of Monmouth. Barbara, Duchess of Cleveland lived in Cleveland House, just off Stable Yard. Initially she lived at Whitehall, but when her rooms were gutted by fire Charles moved her to St James's, where she was hastily housed in the Clock Tower. A few weeks later the King entered her bedroom to find Colonel Churchill, the future Duke of Marlborough, making a hasty retreat from the window. Charles shouted after him as he fled into St James's Street, 'I forgive you, for you do it for your bread'. Indeed, Barbara had been responsible for the dashing Colonel's army promotion. She had blue eyes and blazingly red hair – the King could not resist her. She bore many bastard children, only five of whom Charles recognised as his own: the Dukes of Southampton, Grafton and Northumberland, and the Countesses of Sussex and Lichfield.

The four 'leading ladies' among the mistresses continually gave battle for supremacy. Once, when Nell Gwynne's coach was stopped and jostled by an angry crowd, she opened her window and called out 'but good people, I am the *Protestant whore*', gaining instant laughter.

109. Portrait of Louise de Kerouaille, Duchess of Portsmouth, by Pierre Mignard, 1682.

Nell's story is well known. She began by selling oranges to the audience, and became an experienced actress, entrancing Samuel Pepys, and also Lord Buckhurst, whose mistress she became. The King was infatuated with her, and bought her from Buckhurst for £1,000 a year and a position at court as Groom of the Bedchamber.

Louise de Kerouaille began her affair with Charles whilst he was still in exile. He brought her to London and made her a Maid of Honour to his long-suffering Queen. Undoubtedly she was the most intelligent among these four women, giving the King intellectual, as well as sexual, companionship. She was created Duchess of Portsmouth, and bore Charles a son, Charles Beauclerk, Duke of Richmond.

The fourth lady of the King's pleasure was Hortense Mancini, who became the Duchess of Mazarin. Dark, and smoulderingly beautiful, her greatest rival was the Duchess of Portsmouth. Barbara was quite unassailable with all those children, and bickering was almost friendly with Nell, the little cockney.

James, Duke of York, possessed fewer mistresses than Charles – but certainly not from lack of enthusiasm. It appears that he lacked his brother's wit and charm.

Sadly the joyous romp of Charles's reign had to end. Here are the diarist, John Evelyn's 'Thoughts upon the King at his Death' on 6 February 1685:

> He had a Laboratory, and knew of many empyrical medicines and the easier Mechanical Mathematics. He loved planting, building, and brought in a politer way of living, which passed to Luxurie and intollerable expense. He took delight to have a number of little spaniels to follow him and lie in his bedchamber. This day Sennight, I was witness of the king, sitting and toying with his Concubines, Portsmouth, Cleveland and Mazarin. A French boy, singing love songs in that glorious gallery, whilst about twenty of the great courtiers and other dissolute persons were at Bassett round a large table, a bank of at least £2,000 in gold before them.

We have looked in depth at Charles' passion for women and gambling; this is his popular image through the centuries. Yet there was another man, of forceful action, of physical and moral authority: during the Great Fire of London, Charles gained immense respect from Londoners for his actions.

110.   Portrait of James II by an unknown artist, *c.*1690.

JAMES II

James II's reign was short and ill-starred. During his Coronation, the Crown, when placed upon his head by the Archbishop of Canterbury, slipped sideways and would have fallen had not Henry Sidney stepped forward to make it secure. This incident was taken as an ill omen by the people, and so it proved.

Queen Mary of Modena liked living at St James's Palace. Christopher Wren was building a new Great Drawing Room, and a Great Presence Chamber on the south front, facing the Mall. The King made no secret of his Catholicism, joining his wife openly at Mass in the Queen's Chapel, whereas Charles had been infinitely more circumspect.

Nevertheless, James's position as King was secure enough to cause the utter failure of the Monmouth rebellion that same year (1685). His popularity increased, and encouraged by this he began to put Catholics in positions of power. Indeed, when the French King, Louis XIV, sent James privy warning that William of Orange was planning to land in England, he refused to believe it. William had married Mary, James's eldest daughter by his first wife, Anne Hyde, who had ensured Mary's strong Protestant faith.

And so we come to the bizarre affair of the 'St James's Palace warming pan incident'. With all the building and rebuilding over the years, apartments of royalties and mistresses, doors and back-stairs, secret access to certain bedrooms, and myriad small courtyards, the Palace was by this time a real labyrinth. One observer claimed that 'The Palace was well known to be infested with priests and intriguers, scuttling upon nefarious errands, up and down the secret passages'.

When his Queen became pregnant James was elated, but it was tantamount to putting a flame to a slow-burning fuse. The people feared the birth of an heir to the throne who would undoubtedly be reared as a Catholic. If the pregnancy were pretended, how would, and how *could* a substitute child be arranged? From the first it was thought to be a plot – Mary did not look pregnant, they said – although women's clothes of the period were full and concealing. Many high Church and State officials were required to be present at the birth of any monarch's child, to witness that it was a true heir to the throne. Thus it was that on 10 June 1688 all those dignitaries were required to assemble in the ante-room of the Queen's bedroom when her labour began.

With all the normal scurrying in and out of physicians, midwives and maids, it was yet observed by those dignitaries that a warming-pan was carried past them by a personal attendant to the Queen and taken into the bedroom. This was a utensil used for centuries to warm the cold sheets of a bed before getting in. Imagine two large, deep plates, one covering the other, hinged on one side, secure fastening on the other, and a very long handle, forming a banjo shape. You took small, red hot coals from the fire, slipped them wihin, snapped it shut and then ran it up and down for a few minutes beneath the bedclothes. Warming-pans were normally made of brass, well cleaned and highly polished.

Was a substitute child inside that warming pan? Was a still-born child carried out by one route, a live child brought in by another? They all knew perfectly well of a semi-secret stairway from a small inner courtyard, leading to a door beside the Queen's bed, and it was strongly believed to have been used for the purpose. Whatever the truth of this matter, that child became the 'Pretender', the centre of loyalty for the Jacobites for many years, unavailingly asserting his right to the throne over that of the subsequent monarchs. You will recall from the section on Lancaster House that one theory was that Lady Oglethorpe's child was the substitute, hence her reward of a favourable lease of land at St James's Palace. The bedroom was at the eastern end of the south front on the Mall, a wing subsequently lost in a fire; but William of Orange saw the door by the bed, and confirmed that it opened onto a small stairway.

King James, already disturbed by rumours of William's ships off the south coast, made an announcement decrying suspicions of his heir; condemning 'malicious rumours spread by my enemies' and claiming that 'this child whom God hath pleased to bless me with, scarce any prince was born, where there were so many present'. His protests were of little avail.

William landed on the south coast with 14,000 men. King James left the Palace in great haste to place himself at the head of his army, but the widespread desertion of soldiers, from generals to privates, left him helpless. He returned to St James's Palace, only to discover that his daughter, Princess Anne, had also deserted him. She had left her apartments at night, meeting her childhood friend, Lady Churchill, in the Park, and was spirited away. Her decision to support her sister Mary and brother-in-law William, instead of her father, the King, must have been agonising for her, but it was worse for James. Broken-hearted, he fled the country, and William and Mary's joint monarchy had begun.

WILLIAM AND MARY

On his approach to London, William had spent the night at Syon House on the banks of the Thames, as the guest of the Countess of Northumberland. Upon the information that James had left London, he marched to the capital from the west. His secretary, Huygins, wrote that 'we drove through the gates of Green Park, which His Highness reached at three o'clock, to the loud cheers of the people, a great number with orange ribbons on their hats'. Many of the Londoners were disappointed: they stood in the rain expecting the Prince to drive through Piccadilly, but William was a quiet man, who 'neither loves shows nor shouting', and he asked to be taken the quiet, faster way to St James's Palace, through the park. That route would have been the present Constitution Hill, the centre of Green Park until later years, when George III enlarged Buckingham Palace gardens.

The Prince moved into St James's Palace and made it his headquarters. His bedroom was the very room where James's suspect son had been born – the 'warming-pan room'.

111. Portrait of William III, attributed to Thomas Murray.

112. Portrait of Queen Mary II, after William Wissing.

William and Mary were crowned on 11 April 1689, but rarely came to St James's Palace. William suffered from asthma and found smoky London made him seriously ill. They lived at Hampton Court a great deal of the time, coming to Whitehall for State affairs. Then they bought Kensington Palace, which became their London residence. Fascinating to realise that Kensington was, at that time, outside London, and the air less smoky!

Princess Anne lived in St James's Palace at that time, with her husband, Prince Georg. The two sisters, Mary and Anne, had little love for each other and rarely met. When Mary died, William gave St James's Palace to Anne completely; she remained here when she became Queen – indeed, she was to die here.

On 4 January 1698 a disaster occurred in which London lost centuries of history in stone, wood, brick, records and art treasures. The Palace of Whitehall burned to the ground. A Dutch maid, one of the hundreds of Netherlanders who accompanied William and Mary to London, was drying her linen by the fire in a room lined with panelling. The clothes caught fire, and with incredible speed the fire engulfed the whole Palace. There was a bitter frost, the Thames was frozen over, and firefighters with their primitive apparatus failed to find enough water to be of any use. By the next morning the entire place was a blackened ruin, except, by a miracle, Inigo Jones's most beautiful banqueting house.

From that date St James's Palace became the pre-eminent Palace, the residence of each reigning monarch, until the young Queen Victoria moved into Buckingham Palace. Even then, she continued to use St James's for all State functions and ceremonial. Indeed, many such functions are held here at the present day, and every Ambassador to London is still 'accredited to the Court of St James's'.

After Mary died in 1694, Dutch William continued alone as King for a further eight years. One day, when riding, his horse stumbled over a mole-hill and threw William. He died of his injuries several days later on 8 March 1702. The Jacobites, still plotting to bring the 'Old Pretender' back to the Throne, toasted 'the little gentleman in black velvet', the mole that had killed the Protestant King. But here in St James's Palace waited Anne, with her faithful friends the Churchills.

Let us pause for a moment and consider who was living in St James's Street in 1702 when Anne was proclaimed Queen in Friary Court. There was an inn on the west side, the *Bunch of Grapes*, which advertised 'an extraordinary cask of good, Florence wine at six shillings a gallon'. The first coffee houses were appearing. Mr. Stroud was building Stroud Court, soon to become Pickering Place. In the *Horseshoe* ale house one Simon Weld, obviously a Government spy, reported that 'Cox, a plumber, was heard to speak favourably of James II'. The 'Nags Head' was a 'resort of Jacobites', and, of course, the Cocoa Tree was the nerve centre. All this 'plotting at the very gates of St James's Palace', yet the nobility were also resident here; Sir John Fenwick, Sir Caesar Oranmore, Lady Bellasis. One common lodging house advertised that 'this house is next door to notables'. In other words, St James's Street was a mixture of 'gentry, trade and Inns'.

ANNE

At this time, perhaps more than any other, St James's Palace was truly the centre of the kingdom. Remember, the Palace of Whitehall was no more; on this spot centred the court, the Government and the Civil Service. Queen Anne, with her Consort, Prince Georg of Denmark, lived in the State Apartments. They had many children, none of whom survived infancy. In Godolphin House, now Lancaster House, lived Lord Godolphin with his family; he was Lord Treasurer and an astute politician. Marlborough House, newly built, housed the Churchills, now Duke and Duchess of Marlborough, and their family. His brilliant military victories were financed by Godolphin.

Sarah Jennings had been the Queen's childhood companion. She was a woman of outstanding beauty; her rapport with the plain Anne blossomed into a deep friendship in later years. Sarah married John Churchill, he who leapt out of Barbara's bedroom window whilst he was Charles II's Equerry. When they married, a brilliant future within the court and the army was ensured for them. Sarah became the central figure of society, but her loyalty to the Queen was unquestionable, despite her dominant position in the relationship.

Christopher Wren had by now enlarged the Great Drawing Room and the Great Council Chamber, which he had built for James II on the south front of the Palace, facing The Mall. Beyond them came the Royal Closet, with a staircase to the garden. At this point, Wren created the present Grand Staircase, later completed as it stands today, in a shapely scissor form. The Privy Chamber was next to the Little Drawing Room: beyond that was the State Bedchamber.

Friary Court was still enclosed on the east by the old Tudor 'Queen's side', which comprised two more Drawing Rooms, leading from the Queen's Presence Chamber, a passage room and a writing room. Such was the extent of the old south front that eastward down The Mall there was yet another courtyard where Marlborough Road is today.

The ballroom was west of the Grand Staircase, which today is the Banqueting Hall. The present Ambassadors' Court to the north was still then two smaller courtyards: the inner was Green Cloth Court, the other open to Stable Yard.

Prince Georg had no interest in politics. He was an amiable man who preferred a quiet life with plenty of food and drink, and happy to leave Anne to deal with state functions. Perhaps he found enough interest to appear with the Queen when she received four Red Indian chiefs in full war paint, who brought presents of belts and necklaces, and in return were given Anne's portrait, razors, looking-glasses, scissors and kettles by the Queen, and Bibles by the Archbishop of Canterbury. When the gentle, bibulous Prince Georg died, Anne was desolate. All the doorsteps of the Palace were covered with black flannel, and all the silver sconces and candlesticks were oxidised black. Throughout the whole of that winter those who had to be

113. Painting of Queen Anne with William, Duke of Gloucester, after Sir Godfrey Kneller, *c*.1694.

admitted to the Queen's presence were received in her bedchamber where Anne, dressed in black, sat beside the bed which was covered in purple. No person was admitted if they were not in mourning; this rule applied also to attendance at services in the Chapel Royal.

When Sarah Jennings's impoverished cousin, Abigail Hill, became in need of assistance, Sarah suggested to the Queen that 'Abigail would make a gentle, obedient and efficient personal maid'. The Queen was pleased to have this intimate position filled by her friend's own relation. Sarah's pleasure lay in the knowledge that gratitude would ensure Abigail's compliance with *her* wishes. Abigail's gentle voice and manner, her willingness to obey the Queen's least whim, her proferring of little comforts, all presented a complete contrast to Sarah's demands, quick temper and sarcasm. Anne had always loved the little rooms of St James's Palace, the 'closet rooms', where she felt safe. More and more it became preferable to stay in privacy with Abigail, with little drinks, stools and cushions for comfort. There were fewer 'audiences', where the Marlboroughs and Godolphins advised and demanded decisions. It was slowly realised that this personal maid 'had the queen's ear'.

The rise of Abigail Hill (later Abigail Masham, when she married one of Prince Georg's page boys), had, however, more than a domestic significance. The two major political parties at that time were the Tories and the Whigs. 'High Tories' were Jacobites, mainly landed aristocrats from the shires, whose loyalty lay with the Stuarts and the divine right of kings, who often actively plotted the return of James II. The 'High Fliers' were less convinced in their aims, but had sympathy with the Jacobites. The third element amongst the Tories were the so-called 'Whimsicals', who supported the Hanoverian succession, which eventually acceded to the throne, after Anne's death. The Duke and Duchess of Marlborough and Lord Godolphin were of the last, and dominant group.

The Whigs comprised many of the wealthy bankers and merchants who wanted to wrest political power away from the Tory aristocrats. The Whig most concerned in this Palace affair was Robert Harley, later Lord Oxford, an unprincipled political intriguer, who deserted the Whigs and joined the Tories for the purpose of defeating the powerful Marlborough clique.

Desperately needing access to the Queen for his own purposes, he persuaded Mrs. Masham to smuggle him, via those little stairways and courtyards, to meet Anne in a closet room. How simple it was to flatter the maid, now conscious of her growing power, firstly into arranging brief meetings, assuring the Queen of his loyalty, and going on to induce her to hold full conferences with his associates. Anne, although a staunch Protestant, yearned for her exiled father, James II, whom Harley would extol. Eventually Sarah, alarmed at her cousin's rise to power, attempted to reassert herself. There was a violent quarrel and, although she sent a letter of submission to the Queen, Anne remained adamant, 'requesting the Duchess of Marlborough to leave within two days', and demanding Sarah's gold keys of Office. Sarah at first refused; the Queen then requested the Duke to obtain and return them. He went to Sarah who, after a furious scene, threw them on the floor. He picked them up, walked through the now silent passages to Anne's apartments and returned them to the Queen. When Sarah finally moved her belongings out of her official apartment within the Palace, she tore out the marble mantlepieces and the brass door-locks; if they were installed by the royal locksmith, Josiah Kay, they were worth taking. Kay was famous as the 'most ingenious man in Europe at his craft'.

The manner of Lord Godolphin's dismissal is less well known, but Jonathan Swift wrote: 'A letter from the Queen was sent by the Groom of the Stables, to desire he would break his Staff of Office; Mr. Smith, Chancellor of the Exchequer, happening to call, Godolphin broke the staff, threw the pieces into the fire, asking Smith to witness; and he said: "years of Royal service to end thus; no word of gratitude, no farewell audience"'. So ended the 'Trinity' of those early years of Anne's reign.

Poor Anne, suffering from dropsy, and immensely fat, became virtually a prisoner in later life, as movement became an intolerable burden. In a painting of 1690, one can see a balcony built out from her drawing room on the south front on The Mall, where she could take the air and feel the sunlight. She died in August 1714. The quiet tranquility of those last years contrasts sharply with the vitality, colour and drama of the courts of the Tudors – or the Stuarts, of which line Anne was the last sovereign.

GEORGE I

When George arrived at St James's Palace, among his retinue were two German mistresses, one grossly obese, one thin. Frau Schulenburg became the Duchess of Kendal, and possessed much political influence over George. Frau Kilmenseck became the Countess of Darlington. Both were comfortably ensconsed in apartments in the south front – thus the tradition of Palace courtesans continued. Also among George's household were two Turkish men, Mahomet and Mustapha, captured in Hungary after a batte. They became Pages of the Back-stairs, using these famous secret entries of the Palace for unscrupulous, efficient procuring of anyone or anything.

A day or two after George's arrival, his Germanic sense of possession was somewhat strained. He told a friend that 'I looked out of the window and saw St James' Park with walks, trees and a canal, which they told me were mine. The next day, Lord Chetwynd, Ranger of my Park, sent me a fine brace of carp, out of my canal; and I was told I must give five guineas to Lord Chetwynd's servant – for bringing me my own carp out of my own canal in my own park!'

Each reign added its own memorial in brick and stone at St James's. Records show a new back staircase for the Princess, a parquet floor in Frau Schulenburg's bedroom; the music gallery was redecorated, and an 'engine room' built. The Mews were smartened up and the stables were arcaded. Kitchens and larders were painted, the wainscotting of the royal apartments was thoroughly cleaned and two bedrooms built for the women of the bedchamber in Pheasant Court, which stood where Marlborough Road is today. Later, Grinling Gibbons created doors for the top of that back-staircase leading to Mustapha's bedroom, and he also had a closet room provided.

The reference to an 'engine room' needs explanation. A small courtyard, just off Ambassador's Court, originally called 'Pump' and now 'Engine Court', was the site of the Palace well. Clearly the water was drawn up by hand pump in the earliest years; now George I installed an engine for that purpose. A writer in 1840 recorded that 'There formerly existed in Pump Courtyard, a well of exceptionally good water, which was much prized by the Palace residents and neighbourhood, but it became contaminated and the pump ceased to be used ... It had a long iron handle and stood near the Guardroom, but was lost when the new Guardroom was built. The palace is now supplied with water from the artesian well in Trafalgar Square. An old Palace resident, who remembered the pump many years ago, told me this water was supposed to have medicinal qualities and people came from many parts of the suburbs to obtain it.'

George I had no queen. He had married his cousin, Sophia of Zelle, who committed adultery in a tempestuous affair with Count Konigsmarck, who was later assassinated. George imprisoned Sophia in Castle Ahlen where she eventually died, never again having seen her children. The King had brought his son with him to London, the future George II, whose wife, Caroline, remained in Germany. However,

George needed her as his hostess and she arrived within a few weeks. All the Hanoverian kings hated their first born sons: it runs through their history as a black thread through tapestry. George I's dislike of the Prince of Wales may have stemmed from Sophia's adultery.

The Prince and the Princess could at least speak English. When the King spent a few months in Germany they kept court at St James's Palace in his absence. But the animosity between father and son increased. There were arguments over the Prince's allowance, over the christening of a new born child. The old closet-room passages echoed with furious voices. When the King locked the Prince in his bedroom, the Prime Minister, Sir Robert Walpole, said 'Something *must* be done – the present situation is clearly impossible; the heir to the throne cannot be shut up in his own room like a recalcitrant schoolboy'. The Prince and Princess of Wales were excluded from St James's Palace and allowed to set up their own establishment in Leicester House, at that time north of Leicester Square; and for ten years those out of favour with the King became part of that secondary Court, looking to the future, when the Prince and Princess of Wales would become king and queen. Rewards would then be reaped for loyalty.

Lord Chesterfield commented that: 'George I was an honest, dull, German gentleman, lazy and inactive, even in his pleasures which were lowly sensual. He was coolly intrepid and indolently benevolent. He spoke little in public, preferring his social life which was spent in the company of wags and buffoons. No women came amiss to him if they were both willing and fat'. And Lady Mary Wortley-Montague believed that 'in private life he could have been called a block-head, no man was ever more free from ambition. He spoke no English and was past the age of learning. Our laws and customs were all mysteries to him. Schulenburg was so much of his temper, I don't wonder at the engagement between them'.

The animosity between the King and his son continued. George tried to stop the Prince's allowance but Parliament would not permit this. Walpole again acted as persuasive peacemaker, achieving a degree of harmony for the sake of royal dignity. Princess Caroline was allowed to visit her children: for some time the King had kept them with him at St James's Palace. Caroline became a regular attendant on George's 'Drawing Room Days', but the Prince was still forbidden admittance.

On one of his last visits to Germany the King brought back to the Palace 'the Wild boy', a child found living with the animals in Hamelyn Forest, walking on all fours and completely savage. They had civilised him somewhat, and he appeared in the King's apartments to be shown off to the courtiers and the royal children. He was most at his ease with George, knowing him from their journey together, but refused utterly to sleep in a bed, preferring the floor.

The King had eventually, to the surprise of everyone, especially that of Frau Schulenburg, taken a young English mistress, Anne Brett. Her apartment was on the ground floor of the south front of the Palace, close to that of the Princess Royal. Anne felt that her position was secure enough to order that a door must be cut in her wall, giving immediate access to the garden. The Princess, discovering this, and angry at such undesirable companionship in the garden, countermanded the order: the bricks were to be relaid. Anne, as furiously, demanded that it be opened up again. Spare a thought for the harassed workmen!

The King was en route for Hanover whilst this play was being enacted. The journey was never completed, for he died on the road. The battle between the Princess and the mistress ended, for Anne's days in St James's Palace were over.

The accession of George I to the throne was the last step in the Protestant revolution of 1688. The stability of the Crown may be measured by the utter failure of the Jacobite rebellion in 1715. But this, the first Hanoverian reign, marked the beginning of an age of stability and prosperity for the country. Affection was beginning to appear, very gradually, for the 'German Georges'.

114. Portrait of George II, studio of Charles Jervas, *c.*1727.

GEORGE II

St James's Palace had been unusually quiet during the last years of George I's reign, apart from the turmoil between King and Prince, and Princess and mistress. Glittering social affairs had taken place at Leicester House. Now all was changed. A newspaper said

> The court of George II opens the new year with reckless gaiety that reminds one of the time of Charles II, as described by John Evelyn. Twelfth Night was especially dissipated. There was a ball at St James's Palace and numerous gaming tables. The King and Queen lost five hundred guineas at Ombre, the Earl of Sunderland, twice as much, General Wade lost eight hundred guineas, Lord French, four hundred guineas. The winners were Lord William Manners, one thousand, two hundred, the Duchess of Dorset, nine hundred, and the Earl of Chesterfield, five hundred and fifty guineas. Once again the Palace rings with music and laughter.

The coronation was a magnificent affair, and was followed by a circuit of the royal palaces, as under his father's orders to remain absent from Court, George had scarcely entered many of them. But his great love was St James's Palace, so, removing all his father's mistresses and their retinue forthwith, George II and Queen Caroline moved in. One wonders what happened to Mustapha and Mahomet.

George was an economical man, and possessed a superb memory; an excellent soldier for whom the correct dress was an absolute essential. How many buttons on a uniform, which epaulettes, gloves, swords; all ceremonial was a delight to him. Whilst he was absorbed in these military niceties Queen Caroline and Robert Walpole dealt with Government affairs.

The possessor of an uncontrollable temper, George would kick his hat and wig across the room, but he was also a compassionate man. In his later years a visitor to the Palace, lost among this maze of passages, tripped down a small staircase, hit the door at the bottom and fell unconscious. When he came to 'a severe gentleman with a red face' was carefully washing his bald head, then applied a dressing, and finally replaced his wig for him. It was the King himself.

There were six royal children: Frederick, Prince of Wales, William, Duke of Cumberland, Anne, Caroline, Emily and Louisa. Frederick died before his father (thus his son became George III). The black thread running through the Hanoverians, the hatred (no other word will suffice) of the King for his eldest son, was particularly strong here. It seems, however, that in the case of this Prince of Wales there was some justification for this, to judge by the little satirical verse by which 'Fred' is best remembered today:

> Here lies Fred, who was alive and is dead,
> Had it been his father I had much rather,
> Had it been his brother, still better than another,
> Had it been his sister, no one would have missed her,
> Had it been the whole generation – still better for the nation,
> But since 'tis only Fred,
> Who was alive and is dead,
> There's no more to be said.

Frederick had spent his youthful life almost entirely in Hanover (was parental dislike instrumental in this?) – and it was some years after his father's accession to the throne before he was summoned to St James's Palace. He was taken up to the Queen's apartments by a back stair. Caroline also regarded him with distaste: she called him 'the greatest ass' and George said 'my first born is the greatest beast in all the world'. It comes as no surprise that Frederick took the opposite opinion from his parents on every possible subject.

The King kept a mistress, Amalie Walmoden, in Germany. She had a child who, in later years, after the Queen's death, came to St James's Palace with his mother. This caused an embarrassing scene for Lord Chesterfield, Secretary of State, when he saw 'a well-dressed boy, who seemed to be completely at home in the Palace'; he 'gave much gushing attention with glowing compliments to his mother. The boy listened with becoming gravity and then said "I believe you take me for Master Louis [George's bastard son], but I am Sir William Russell, one of the Pages".' George's English mistress was Mrs. Howard, an intelligent, witty woman, whose salon attracted Pope, Gay and Jonathan Swift. Early in this affair Mr. Howard, in a fine rage, decided not to be a complacent cuckold, stormed into an inner Palace courtyard and loudly shouted demands for the return of his wife forthwith. He was 'ejected and soothed with a pension of £1,200 a year'. Mrs. Howard, eventually created Countess of Suffolk, lived in the same set of apartments as had George I's mistress, Frau Schulenburg.

A fantastic episode in the Palace history occurred during this reign. The Lady Diana Spencer, daughter of Charles Spencer and Lady Anne Churchill, grand-daughter of Sarah, Duchess of Marlborough (who was still living in Marlborough House, watching the new Hanoverians with avidity), almost married Frederick, Prince of Wales! Old Sarah promoted this with all her conniving ability and almost succeeded, but the Lady Diana showed little interest in poor Fred, and married instead the Duke of Bedford. How Sarah must have raged! And with what delight, if she is looking down on St James's Palace in the 1980s, must she have greeted the marriage of Lady Diana Spencer to Charles, Prince of Wales.

The petty harassment of Frederick by the King continued. His servants were not permitted to collect ice from the frozen lake in the park (the ice was much prized in those times of no refrigerators, and 'ice-houses', half underground, were used to store it for as long as possible). Royal courtiers and doctors were forbidden to dine with him. Eventually, the King realised, his dislike nothwithstanding, that Frederick, as Prince of Wales, should be married. Casting his eye over all eligible young women in Europe, they chose Princess Augusta of Saxe-Gotha, who arrived on 25 April 1736 at Greenwich, travelled by river to Whitehall and was driven across the park to the Garden Stairs of the Palace. Taken into the presence of the King and Queen a few hours later, she curtsied most deeply to her future in-laws, having been advised it would please the protocol-minded King, and pave the way for a better relationship between George and the Prince and Princess of Wales.

The marriage took place in the Chapel Royal; all went extremely well, and for once this royal family united on a happy occasion. This was followed by that other, more archaic, ceremony, the 'Bedding' of the newly-wed couple. The bride was taken to her bedroom with her Woman of the Bedchamber and maids, who undressed her with much gentle teasing, and put on a nightdress more suitable for a Ball, then tucked her into the bed, also adorned with rich hangings. The groom was escorted to his apartment by his well-dined and wined friends where they, and the valet, among much bawdy laughter, undressed the groom, arrayed him in a 'nightgown of silver stuff and a lace cap'. Whence they all proceeded in an hilarious procession – in which the King joined – to poor Augusta's bedroom, where Frederick was installed in bed at his bride's side. For the next hour they were on show, sitting beneath the bed canopy, receiving compliments, advice, and more wine, after which they were finally left to their night's pleasure.

Within a short time Augusta became pregnant. When the King and, more especially, the Queen, made it known that they fully intended to be present at the birth of their grandchild, Frederick determined they would not. As the time approached the court was temporarily at Hampton Court. When Augusta's pains began in earnest it was late at night and everyone had retired to their rooms. Fred forced his pathetic princess to walk downstairs to a coach, supported by Lady Archibald Hamilton, her Lady-in-Waiting, Mrs. Payne and Mrs. Clavering, her maids, Frederick's valet, Vried, and Bloodworthy, his Equerry.

They drove frantically to St James's Palace, which was shattered out of a quiet night's sleep to receive the Prince and Princess, and make all ready for the birth. 'No fine sheets to be found' and tablecloths were used for Augusta's bed! There was an urgent search for Officers of State who were required to be present at a royal birth. No Lords of the Council were available, but Lord Godolphin, still living in his house at the Palace, and Lord Wilmington were present when the child was born. Only then was a message sent to Hampton Court informing the King and Queen of the bizarre event.

George II and Caroline were overall somewhat unlucky with their children. Princess Caroline 'was known to have fallen hopelessly in love with Lord Hervey; on his death she shut herself up in two rooms, opening into a small inner courtyard of the Palace, and in religious seclusion she prepared for death'.

Their second son, William, Duke of Cumberland, a somewhat brutal military man, was to become infamous as that bane of the Scots, 'The Butcher' of the Jacobite rising in 1745. In his youth he was given instruction in chemistry amongst other subjects. He set up a laboratory in the Palace cellars, arousing fear in case the young Prince should blow up the royal family; so the Treasury provided him with a larger, more convenient, laboratory at Richmond.

Princess Anne was married to the Prince of Orange in the Chapel Royal in 1734. He was badly deformed. Lord Hervey, asked for an opinion, assured the Queen – 'it was not as bad as she had imagined, his figure was appalling but his face agreeable'. Caroline refused to favour the union. After the wedding she said privately to Lord Harvey 'My God, when I saw this monster come to sleep with my daughter, I thought I would die'. Yet the Princess, like so many others in the 18th century, bore deep scars from smallpox on her face.

On 20 November 1739 Queen Caroline died, after a long and painful illness. Lord Hervey, present in the Queen's bedroom to the end, tells us: 'The King was in furious tears, Caroline comforting him. She insisted he should remarry. "No, no", he protested, "I shall take mistresses"; "that makes no difference" came the emphatic answer.' He did not remarry, but he brought Amalie Walmoden with their son to St James's Palace.

When Amalie Walmoden arrived here from Hanover, she was entitled the Countess of Yarmouth and given the set of rooms which George's father's mistress, the Duchess of Kendal (Frau Schulenburg) had had, and she became as powerful as Kendal had been in George I's reign. Yet a family atmosphere prevailed. The King played cards with his daughters in Amalie's apartment each evening, with little suppers and much laughter. A writer of 1868, sharing my interest in the domestic affairs of St James's Palace, states:

> Enough has been narrated to show that the Palace, though dull to outward appearance, has witnessed merry doings within its walls. Somewhat incline they did to romping. The Countess of Huntingdon desperately tried to establish a Mission within these walls, making an impression upon only one Maid of Honour. What this pious lady could not do was accomplished under the watchful and wary eye of George III's consort in the next reign.

The final curtain for this second Hanoverian king fell in 1760. 'Death came to George, wearing the cap and bells of low comedy, for this, like other crises in his life, was coloured by farce. He rose at his normal hour of 6 a.m., called for his chocolate, and repaired, as usual to his closet stool [lavatory]. The Valet de Chambre, hearing a noise, then a groan, rushed in and found him lying on the floor. Walpole though it "an enviable death, to die without a pang".' Once again a King's mistress departed from St James's Palace; and the 'old order' changed dramatically in the next reign!

GEORGE III

George III, poor Fred's son, succeeded to the throne as a young man of 22 years. He had a long reign, for he died in 1820, but for the last ten years his son ruled as Regent, a situation necessitated by the King's complete mental breakdown.

In 1760 all was happy and optimistic. Going through George II's papers, the young King found that 6,000 guineas were to be given to Lady Yarmouth, his father's mistress. To this he added 2,000 guineas, and Amalie retired gracefully, with excellent provision for her welfare. Apart from an early – and unavailing – passion for Lady Sarah Lennox, Charles II's granddaughter by the Duchess of Portsmouth, George III never even considered taking a mistress, in a complete reversal of Hanoverian custom. St James's Palace was to be ruled by a benevolent matriarchal domesticity for many years, marred only by the king's malady at the end of his reign.

George found the Palace neglected and comfortless. Upstairs Queen Caroline's bedroom was still preserved. In 1758 Sir Robert Walpole saw lying in the hearth the wood laid for her fire the day she died, 21 years before! George stripped the Queen's old ground-floor rooms on the south front and in three years they were converted into a library.

When George married Princess Charlotte of Mechlenburg-Strelitz, further renovation took place. The Yeoman Tailor, Paul Saunders, cleaned the tapestries with bran; the embroideress, Mrs. Sarah Green, made a crimson velvet canopy for their bed. 'Each day, the Lord Steward's department dispensed a livery of wax and tallow', that is, white waxen candles for the superb silver candlesticks and sconces in the royal apartments, which were decorated in gold and blue. Tallow candles were used for all other rooms.

Charlotte's bedroom was hung with pale blue silk. Her sitting room was the 'Bow Room'. Horace Walpole remembered the 'room with the bow window, looking onto Marlborough House'.

Charlotte bore 15 living children, nine sons and six daughters. After the birth of their first child she ate only 'caudle' for a few days – crumbled bread, with hot milk poured over, eggs, wine and a little spice beaten in. Guests honoured by a visit to the newborn Prince of Wales (the future George IV) also ate caudle or a little cake.

With an ever-growing family, George bought Buckingham House for £28,000 from Sir Charles Sheffield, the Duke of Buckingham's son. This became a private home, while St James's Palace was still used for all official affairs. The King said 'Buckingham House was not meant for a Palace but a retreat'. Eventually, completely rebuilt, it was to become Buckingham Palace. One reason for the royal family's change of residence was that St James's was proving too easy for the uninvited to infiltrate. The original Tudor plan for Henry VIII – the Gatehouse and the enclosed Friary Court, with King's wing and Queen's wing, east and west, which had formed an easily-patrolled and defensible shape – had been lost over the centuries by alterations.

Nevertheless, St James's was still very much lived-in. There were large, hair-filled cushions on the floor for the dogs (the Queen's was called 'Presto'); William Vile made 'an Exceeding fine Mahogany Secretary, with cuttwork sides' for £71; also elaborate stands for the children's goldfish bowls. The Queen played the harpsichord in the Music Room, where she was also taught singing by J. C. Bach.

George and Charlotte lived very simply and ate small meals – rarely more than three courses in this age of over-indulgence. They were very strict with their children, who were to rise at 7.30 a.m. and have one hour of tuition before breakfast. This quiet, family life, was in great contrast to the far more flamboyant Court of the French King and Queen, Louis XVI and Marie Antoinette, on the other side of the Channel. When the French Revolution broke out and Louis was deposed, George and Charlotte became even more popular in the country. When, in 1788, George's mental instability first briefly appeared, the people were genuinely concerned; on the King's improvement a few months later there was great relief and much rejoicing.

On one occasion at least, the King's life was endangered by his coachman. At 'the angle from Cleveland Row into Stable Yard, the hind wheel of the coach hit the post at the corner of the footpath leading to Stafford House [now Lancaster House]. The shock tore up three paving stones, broke a sway-bar, and threw the coachman off the box.' Perhaps this is the reason for the rounding of that corner-wall of York House. It is still an awkward entrance today.

There were several attempts upon the King's life, all of which failed (see p. 67 above). 'I very well know that any man who chooses, may take away my life – I only hope in not too barbarous and brutal a manner', said the King.

In 1810 occurred one of the most bizarre events in the history of St James's Palace. The Duke of Cumberland, the King's third son, became the victim of an attempted assassination by his valet, who then committed suicide. Here are some extracts of *The Times* report of the affair:

ATTEMPT AT ASSASSINATION
ONE OF THE MOST EXTRAORDINARY EFFORTS EVER MADE TO COMMIT THIS DIABOLICAL CRIME

Soon after midnight, His Royal Highness, the Duke of Cumberland, returned to his apartment in Kitchen Court, St James's Palace; at 2.30 a.m., was awakened by blows to his temple by a sabre; he grappled with his assailant, wrenched the sabre from his grasp – the attacker fled. The alarm was raised – Robbers? A Sergeant of the Guard with five men entered, went upstairs to the bedroom – the stairs were covered in blood, as the Duke had gone down to call for the Porter and a light. Royal doctors gave assistance, Sir Henry Halford and Mr. Home, Surgeon ...

On searching, no trace of the assassin was found by the Guards, until they came to Seillis's room, where they found the miserable wretch on the bed, dressed, except for coat, waistcoat and shoes, head nearly severed from the body – and a razor, the instrument of suicide, beside him. The body quite dead, and had been so for many minutes before. Seillis is a Valet, and Italian. The Duke has three such men about him, Neale is English. Seillis left a wife and four children, the eldest eight years: he was a favourite of the Duke, and been with him for almost ten years, and lived over the gateway into Kitchen Court in rooms communicating with the Duke's apartments. Seillis, is in some sort, an object of particular attention to all the Royal Family.

On the Duke's getting out of bed, he shouted 'Neale, Neale, I am murdered'. Neale was instantly awake; armed with a poker he and the Duke went along the passage. Neale stepped on a sword which was the Duke's regimental sabre and had been

114

sharpened. Both woke the house. The Duke and Neale, without suspicion, knocked on Seillis's door, who, it was supposed, mistook what was said, viz: 'Seillis, the Duke has been murdered' for 'Seillis, you have murdered the Duke'. It is *then* supposed he concluded he was detected, as he was heard opening the drawer in which was the razor. Lieutenant Buller, a Sergeant, and several men entered, and found Seillis dead.

The Duke's statement was as follows:

> I awoke at three o'clock to violent blows and a hissing noise, and thought a bat was in the room; a lamp was burning – by the light I saw a letter on the table covered in blood – thought the murderer in the room; I struggled out of bed and saw a man flying out of the room.

Seillis had, apparently, been incensed by the Duke's deciding against him in a domestic dispute. The Duke's head wounds were serious; 'the brain could be seen, pulsating – also his neck, thigh and right thumb were cut'.

On the next day 'The body of Seillis was buried yesterday in Scotland Yard, in the highway toward the Thames, about two yards before the door of the Egg Warehouse'.

A disastrous fire occurred in 1809; the whole south wing was destroyed, including the Tudor range. Gone were the rooms of the warming-pan affair in James II's reign; the Queen's drawing room and bedroom, the last traces of the Old Friary. Queen's Chapel was miraculously untouched, indeed, furniture and valuables were taken there for storage.

No special quarters had ever been made available for the Guards. Indeed, there are indications of the Chapel Royal being used for this purpose, before Charles I's restoration work on it. In 1793 the King ordered a guard room to be built in Engine Court, and a meal provided for the men whilst on duty. This remained in use for almost a century, despite constant complaints of bad drainage. Remember the well in this little court? Even sealed off, it must have caused dampness.

The names of the many court officials give us some idea of the Palace's complex and fascinating organisation: there were the Masters of Ceremonies, the Jewel Office, the Great Wardrobe, the Horse, Harriers and Buckhounds; below them a host of others such as the Table Decker, Deliverer of Greens, Spatterdash Maker, Sedan-chair Maker, Sempstress, Body Laundress, Rat-catcher, Mole-taker, Bug-taker and a splendid personage known as the 'Embellisher of Letters to Eastern Princes'. Lastly, we cannot forget the Cock of the Court, as he called the hours in the Courtyard – 'three o'clock and all's well'.

The King's periods of insanity became more frequent; people in the street stopped the doctor's coach, asking with immense concern how the patient fared. In 1810 the death of his daughter, Princess Amelia, finally tipped the balance. He became irrevocably mad, and eventually blind. The Prince of Wales was appointed Prince Regent in 1811.

The unfortunate King finally died in 1820. Jermyn Street and St James's were filled with French families who had fled from the terror of the guillotine. The next two sovereigns were both old men with brief reigns. In Kensington Palace a baby girl, named Victoria, was one year old.

GEORGE IV

On 29 January 1820, when the old King died, the Proclamation of Accession was, as always, made at St James's Palace. George IV was in Brighton, too ill to travel. His doctors used the old practice of blood-letting; and, having lost 80 ounces, George improved sufficiently to return to London.

St James's was still the centre of state affairs, drawing-rooms, balls and receptions. The King held more personal festivities here, too, such as the annual Jockey Club dinners. On 28 May 1829 he held one of the many Children's Balls. Greville was present and tells us:

> I saw for the first time the ten-year-old Queen of Portugal, and our little Victoria (our future Queen). The Queen was finely dressed, with a Riband and Order on her shoulder, and she sat by the King. She is good looking and the King was kind to her. Our little Princess is a short, plain-looking child, not near so good looking as the Portuguese. However, if nature had not done so much for her, fortune is likely to do a good deal more.

Nevertheless George IV continued to spend a great deal of his time at Carlton House and at his fantastic Pavilion at Brighton. Mrs. Fitzherbert was, of course, the great love of George's life whom he married morganatically in secret. Their long liaison scarcely belongs to St James's, as do the previous royal loves, but to Brighton. In later years there were other mistresses, notably Lady Jersey of whom more later.

None of George III's sons had a legal heir, though many bastards. George had married Caroline of Brunswick, upon which drama I shall presently enlarge; and when their only child, Charlotte, died tragically in 1817, there ensued a sudden flurry of weddings among the royal princes, a race to produce an heir to the throne. The Duke of Clarence married Adelaide of Saxe-Coburg, but their children died in infancy. The second son, the Duke of York, died childless. The Duke of Kent sadly forsook his mistress, Madame St Laurent, and married Victoria May Louise, widow of the Prince of Leiningen and the daughter of the Saxe-Coburgs. They had one child, Victoria, who became Queen after the deaths of her uncles, King George IV and King William IV.

George had married Caroline whilst he was still Prince of Wales. The wedding took place in the Chapel Royal at St James's Palace in 1795; the couple had not previously met. It was a complete disaster. The prince was at that time in the throes of love with Lady Jersey, a fascinating and lovely woman; the contrast between this bewitcher and Caroline – an earthy woman with bad manners and doubtful habits in matters of hygiene – was altogether too much for him. Nevertheless they produced their one child, Charlotte. Caroline lived abroad, separated from her husband. When George became King she returned to London, demanding to be recognised as Queen, with the attendant status and privileges. George spent many years energetically opposing this, which culminated in a trial by the House of Lords. During the trial Caroline attended Parliament daily, driving from her rented house in St James's Square by carriage. The King's own dissolute way of life created a wave of sympathy for Caroline, but she could not get her way. She died three years later.

George IV, always enthusiastic over architecture and interior decoration, was busy at St James's Palace. He caused the blackened ruins caused by the fire to be removed,

115. The trial of Queen Caroline in the House of Lords, painted by George Hayter, 1820.

and built the beautiful Banqueting Room. Nash, the architect, was later to rebuild Buckingham Palace – he also created Regent Street.

One of the highlights in the long life of the Palace came in 1814, with Napoleon's defeat and exile to Elba. Ambassador's Court was bustling with activity. The Tzar of Russia came to London, as did the King of Prussia who stayed in Clarence House; and Marshal Blucher had apartments in a house on the west side of Ambassador's Court.

There was a Grand Jubilee for the state visit of the Allied Sovereigns; the trees in St James's Park and Green Park were hung with lanterns, the bridge was built over the lake with the Chinese pagoda. There were booths selling souvenirs and firework displays. The celebrations went on for days. The clubs and shops in St James's Street and Pall Mall were filled with revellers, spending money eagerly. Napoleon's escape from Elba put an abrupt end to these celebrations: yet within a year they would be renewed, after Wellington's triumph at Waterloo.

During the last years of George IV's life he became bloated, suffering from dropsy and heart disease. He died on 25 May 1830. An immense collection of clothes, canes, whips and boots was found in his various wardrobes in London and Brighton, for he threw nothing away. More than £10,000 was hidden in wallets and boxes about his apartments; there were all sorts of oddments, ladies' gloves, scarves, trinkets, lockets with curls of hair and protestations of love; jewels and beautiful snuff boxes.

WILLIAM IV

William IV, George III's third son, known as the Sailor King, was a rollicking, generous, outspoken man; yet he had served under Nelson, and his naval training meant he had an unexpected ability to get to the root of any problem. When he became King his ministers were pleasantly surprised by his confidence and common-sense. The arranged marriage with Princess Adelaide had failed in its purpose to provide an heir to the throne, but the King and Queen lived at St James's Palace in friendly domesticity, the young Princess Victoria waiting in the wings.

On the day of his accession, when William arrived at the Palace to hear the Royal Proclamation, huge crowds were waiting in Friary Court for the Herald to appear. Court officials decided to clear the courtyard. Bluff William asked in great surprise 'where are all the people?' and ordered the gates opened forthwith, and the crowds roared back inside with cheers.

William and Adelaide settled down in St James's Palace with a simple daily routine. The diarist Greville recorded that 'he sleeps in the same room with the Queen; at 7.45 a.m. each morning, his Valet de Chambre knocks at the door, and at 7.50 a.m. exactly, he gets out of bed, puts on a flowered dressing gown and trousers, walks into his Dressing-room. He is long at his ablutions, up to an hour and a half. At 9.30 precisely, he takes breakfast with the Queen'. Another writer, Creevey, tells us: 'William and Adelaide only want to be comfortable, and were quite willing to continue at St James's Palace provided some adjacent home might be found, as it was inconvenient to be obliged to move all their books, papers, etc., out of their Sitting room and Drawing room, every levee day, because these rooms are wanted on such occasions. As for removing to Buckingham Palace, he will do so if the Government wish it, though he thinks it a most ill contrived house, and if he goes there, he hopes it may be *plain* and no gilding, for he dislikes it extremely.' Creevey continued: 'the King had a further idea. What he *would* prefer, would be living in Marlborough House, if he might have a passage made to unite that house with St James's. He thinks he and the Queen could live there very comfortably.'

Greville's diary reveals an affection for William IV, similar to that of an uncle for an unruly nephew. On 20 July 1830 he wrote 'He *must* needs put on his plain clothes, and start on a ramble about the streets, all alone, too. In Pall Mall, he met Watson Taylor, took his arm and went up St James's Street. There, he was soon followed by a mob making an uproar and when he got near White's, a whore came up and kissed him. Belfast and Clinton, who saw this from White's, thought it time to interfere, and came out to attend him. The mob increased, and always holding Taylor's arm, flanked by Clinton and Belfast, who got shoved and kicked about, to their inexpressible wrath. He got back to the Palace amid shouting and bawling and applause. He said "oh, never mind all this, when I have walked about a few times they will get used to it, and take no notice".'

It was to this plain-spoken King that the inhabitants of St James's Street appealed when the clock which they found so useful was removed from the Great Gatehouse in 1830. The Great Gatehouse had borne a clock for at least 350 years. There is a print of 1638, when Marie de Medici arrived to visit Charles I and Henrietta Maria, showing a clock face on the tower. By 1731 the great clock was installed, with a bell which was inscribed 'Clay, Clockmaker to George II, A.D. 1731'. A hundred years later this clock was taken down for repair and not replaced, on the assumption that the roof could not take the weight, due to age. The residents of St James's Street, missing the mellow chimes, petitioned William for its return. The King asked the Clerk of the Works why. On being given the reason, he demanded to know why 'if the roof was unsafe for a clock, how could it take the weight of the masses of people who climbed up there on levee and Drawing-room days, to watch to the comings and goings of the famous faces?' The clock was restored immediately.

William had a great affection for his niece, Princess Victoria, and great dislike of her mother, that princess who had married the Duke of Kent during the royal flush of weddings in 1817. The Duchess of Kent dominated her daughter and kept her in over-strict seclusion at Kensington Palace. The King demanded the presence of Victoria at his drawing-rooms and expressed the hope: 'I trust my life will be spared until Victoria comes of age, and no Regency be necessary'. On Victoria's 14th birthday, 24 May 1833, the King gave a Ball at St James's Palace in her honour, personally leading her in the dance. She sat between the King and Queen at dinner. In July 1835 the young princess was confirmed in the Chapel Royal; the Archbishop 'frightened her almost to tears', but she wrote in her diary 'he did everything very well'. She wore a white lace dress, and a white bonnet encircled with flowers.

In May 1837 William attended his last reception at St James's Palace. He looked tired; indeed he sat most of the time, looking very old. He 'wanted to live a few more weeks for the glorious anniversary of Waterloo' on 18 June, which he managed to see. He also saw Victoria's coming of age. He died on 20 June 1837 amid very genuine national grief. The long Victorian era had begun.

116. 'The throne investiture' of Victoria: an engraving by Melville and Gilbert.

VICTORIA

In the early hours of the morning of William's death the Archbishop of Canterbury and Lord Conyngham hastened to Kensington Palace with the news. No-one had yet stirred out of bed. Victoria, woken by her mother, appeared in her dressing-gown. The next day the Queen drove to St James's Palace to hear the Proclamation in Friary Court, the third in the short time of 26 years. There was not to be another for 64 years. The streets about the palace were solid with people, eager to see their new sovereign of whom they knew so little. The talk in the Clubs, Inns and shops of St James's Street and Pall Mall was all of her fresh youth.

As guns were fired in salute from the park, Victoria appeared at the Privy Council Chamber windows, surrounded by her ministers. Lord Albemarle, among the crowds, wrote 'Never shall I forget the enthusiastic cheers which greeted the slight, girlish figure, nor the thrill of chivalrous loyalty that ran through the assembled multitude'. At 12 o'clock that day she presided at a Council with as much ease as if she had been doing it all her life; after which she received the Archbishops and Bishops, to whom she said nothing, but showed an extreme dignity and gracefulness of manner. Ceremony at an end, she retired with slow stateliness; but, forgetting that the door had glass panels, she was seen 'scampering away like a child released from school'.

Queen Victoria lived her domestic life at Buckingham Palace, with St James's Palace still used as the setting for all State functions and ceremonial. In 1840, having proposed to her beloved Prince Albert, she decided that the wedding should take place at St James's Palace, in the ancient Chapel Royal where she had been confirmed. They spent the previous night here in readiness for the ceremony: the Duchess of Kent thought it 'indelicate' that they slept under the same roof before their wedding. For the ceremony the Queen wore white satin with Honiton lace, a diamond necklace and earrings, also a superb sapphire brooch from Prince Albert. There were 12 bridesmaids, each carrying white roses.

Baron Stockmar now enters the picture. He had been instrumental, via Leopold, King of the Belgians, in bringing Victoria and Albert together. To say he became the perfect Secretary is understating the case; he was utterly efficient and omnipresent in their lives. From Stockmar we learn a great deal of the extraordinary confusion of administrative duties, within and without this Palace, which had grown immeasurably worse with the years.

In the time of George I in 1714 the Lord Steward had charge of the whole Palace inside, except the Royal Apartments, which were the province of the Lord Chamberlain. During George IV and William IV's reigns, the Lord Steward attended only to the ground floor. Now, in the 1840s, the Lord Steward surrenders to the Lord Chamberlain the ground floor also, but whether kitchens, pantries, still-rooms etc. were yet the Lord Steward's, nobody knew.

Outside the Palace the Office of Woods and Forests were responsible. That is, they were responsible for the parks, the gardens, obviously with the courtyards and stables, and the outside walls and windows, but the Lord Chamberlain's men cleaned *inside* the windows. The housekeeper, maids, dressers and pages were within the Lord Chamberlain's province; the footmen, porters, coachmen and stablemen were under the Master of the Horse. The Clerk of the Kitchen, the cooks, kitchen women and hall porters came under the Lord Steward. Thus, when the Queen asked why the fire in the Drawing room was not lit, an official of the Lord Steward's department said 'Properly speaking, it is not our fault, for the Lord Steward *lays* the fire only, the Lord Chamberlain lights it'. Today's trade union demarcation rules pale into insignificance!

Should any item become broken, lost or unfit for use, this was the correct procedure (let us suppose a saucepan was required). The Chief Cook signed a requisition form, which was countersigned by The Clerk of the Kitchen. This piece of paper went to the Master of the Household, upon his approbation, to the Lord Chamberlain's office for authorisation. From there it went to the Clerk of the Works at, of course, the Ministry of Works. So the poor Cook, working without his saucepan, waited in frustration, probably for months – we all know how bureaucracy

117. The Guard Chamber at St James's Palace, painted by Charles Wild.

works. Informed of this state of affairs, Prince Albert set about reorganisation with an immense zest, and with Stockmar's efficient assistance. He began in 1842 at Windsor Castle as well as at St James's Palace; 'the elimination of waste, muddle and mismanagement was not completed until 1846'. How greatly they must have enjoyed creating a simple, orderly, logical routine, and gained much gratitude from the bewildered staff.

The early Victorians seem to have been deeply aware of the ancient history of St James's Palace. Many factual books were published in this period. Take Curling's *Some Account of the Ancient Corps of the Gentlemen-at-Arms*, which gives us this picture of the scene during the time when there were fears of a Chartist uprising, on 10 April 1848.

> Colour Court was 'filled' with armed men, and its Chambers and passages, glittering with the bright weapons of the various Guards, some of whom were to be seen passing up and down in the same costume in which their predecessors had mounted Guard when the Royal Tudor sat in aweful Majesty over three hundred years ago. The Gates under the Clock Tower were closed, and a platform built at the back of the Gates, over which the soldiers could fire up St James's Street. Except on this occasion, these Gates have never been closed.

In the event, the Palace was never in danger, and soldiers did not fire up St James's Street.

The Gates of which Curling spoke are the ones where the two Guards stand duty today. They lead into Colour Court. In these modern times those Gates are always closed; and the old entrance to Ambassador's Court, an ancient archway standing alongside, has also been closed by a pair of matching gates. A sad indication of that present-day essential – security.

Prince Albert died in 1861, and Victoria, in the long years of her grieving seclusion, came rarely to St James's Palace. We know of her visits to the Duke and Duchess of Sutherland at Stafford House (now Lancaster House). Also, of course, to the Prince and Princess of Wales at Marlborough House, where 'Bertie and Alex' were the centre of London's social life. Upon Queen Victoria's death in 1901 they moved to Buckingham Palace as King Edward VII and Queen Alexandra, whilst the Prince and Princess of Wales went from York House – named for them while Duke and Duchess of York – into Marlborough House.

THE TWENTIETH CENTURY

When King Edward VII died in 1910, his widow, Queen Alexandra, returned to Marlborough House, whilst the new King, George V, with his wife, Queen Mary, moved into Buckingham Palace. In 1919 their eldest son, Edward, Prince of Wales, took up residence at York House. When King George V died in 1936, Queen Mary went back to Marlborough House; Edward became King Edward VIII for a short period only. When he abdicated in 1937 his younger brother acceded to the throne as King George VI and took up residence at Buckingham Palace with his lovely Queen Elizabeth.

When their daughter, the Princess Elizabeth, married Prince Philip, their married life began at Clarence House. Upon King George VI's death in 1952 Queen Elizabeth II and Prince Philip, Duke of Edinburgh, moved into Buckingham Palace, whilst Queen Elizabeth, the Queen Mother, took up residence in Clarence House.

The damage caused by air-bombing during World War II was surely the most shattering event in the life of this old Palace. On 15 October 1940 a landmine exploded by the railings in St James's Park, damaging windows in the State Apartments, Ambassador's Court, Clarence House, Engine Court and Friary Court. On 10 November 1940 a bomb fell in Cleveland Row, causing structural damage to York House. On 5 March 1941 many incendiary devices fell on the roofs of the Guardroom in Engine Court, York House and Clarence House: through the vigilance of the faithful firewatchers there was no major fire damage. Lastly, on 10 May 1941, a high-explosive bomb fell near Friary Court, causing a great deal of damage, even to the Great Gate-Tower.

POSTSCRIPT

Two last voices speak from the past. Firstly, John Gerard, the celebrated herbalist in Queen Elizabeth I's reign in the earliest years of the 16th century, tells us of the plants he found, growing wild in his London, reminding us that the Tudor St James's was a rural retreat:

> I have found mallow, shepherd's purse, sweet woodruff, bugle and St Paul's Betany; and in the meadows are red-flowered clary, white saxifrage, the sad coloured rocket, yarrow, lesser hawk-weed, strawberry-headed trefoil, wallflowers, and golden stone-crop about the houses. In my own garden, double-flowered peach and wild thyme; these be strangers in England, yet I have them.

He was one of the earliest to grow the potato in London; and when he left his beloved garden to walk in the streets he found:

> Little wild buglosse in the dry ditches around Piccadillo, vervain mallow on the ditch-sides on the left-hand of the place of execution called Tyburn; Hemlock among the ossiers above the Horse-Ferry against Lambeth; chickweed spurrey in the sandy ground in Tothill Fields nigh unto Westminster; pimpernel-rose in the pasture as you go from a village hard by London called Knights Bridge, and silver cinque foil upon brick and stone walls about London, partridge and pheasant upon the wing at Charing Cross and St Martin's Lane.

Finally, the verdict of a jury, visiting the Hospital of St James's in the reign of Edward III (1327-1377), recites the story of St James's earliest days:

> They say the Hospital was founded on two hides of land on the village of Westminster, under the Parish of St Margaret, by certain citizens of London, before the time of records, the names of the citizens are unknown. These lands are held from the Abbott on terms of fealty and suit at his Court of Westminster, the tenure terminable at three weeks notice, at payment of seven solidi and eight denarii a year. And the said Hospital was founded for fourteen sisters, leprouse women, and virgins, to live in chastity and good repute in the Service of God.

For over four hundred and fifty years this Palace of St James's has sheltered our sovereigns, and so many other different lives. The author hopes that this book will have done something to dispel ignorance about the Palace and give all visitors to St James's, British or foreign, a glimpse of the central role this small area and its ancient palace have played in the history of our nation.

Bibliography

Allen, J. Warner, *Number 3 St. James's Street*, Chatto and Windus, 1956

Andrews, A, *Follies of Edward VII*, Lexington, 1975

Bald, R. C., *John Donne: A Life*, Oxford, 1970

Bell, W. E., *Great Fire of London*, Bodley Head, 1921

Beer, E. S. de (ed.), *Diary of John Evelyn*, Oxford, 1955

Besant, W., *London*, Chatto and Windus, 1892

Brooke, C. N. L. & Keir, G, *London 800-1216: The Shaping of a City*, Secker & Warburg, 1975

Buchan, John, *Oliver Cromwell*, Hodder & Stoughton, 1934

Burke, T., *Streets of London*, Batsford, 1940

Burnett, Bishop, *History of My Own Time*, 1723

Chancellor, B. E., *Private Palaces of London*, Kegan Paul, 1908

Chancellor, B. E., *Memorials of St. James's Palace*, 1922

Churchill, W., *History of the English-Speaking People*, Cassell, 1956-8

Cowie, L. W., *Hanoverian England 1741-1837*, Bell, 1967

Cunningham, P., *Handbook of London*, Murray, 1849

Dasent, A. J., *Lancaster House*, Murray, 1921

Dasent, A. J., *Private Life of Charles II*, Cassell, 1927

Deacon, R., *History of the British Secret Service*, Muller, 1969

Ditchfield, P. H., *Memorials of Old London*, Bemrose & Sons, 1908

Dobson, A. (ed.), *Diary and Letters of Fanny Burney*, Macmillan, 1904

Doran, J., *Life in the Jacobite Times*, Bentley & Sons, 1877

Fisher, G. & H., *Bertie and Alix: Anatomy of a Royal Marriage*, Ulverscroft Large Print Books, 1975

Fitz Stephen, W., *Life of Thomas à Beckitt*, 1723

Frewin, L. & B., *Bucks and Bawds of London Town*, Allen Lane, 1974

Fulford, R., *George IV*, Ducksworth, 1935

Fulford, R., *Royal Dukes*, Ducksworth, 1935

Green, D., *Queen Anne*, 1970

Grey, E. C. W., *St. Giles of the Lepers*, Longman Green, 1905

Halsband, R. (ed.) *Complete Letters of Lady Mary Wortley Montagu*, Oxford, 1955

Hedley, O., *Queen Charlotte*, Murray, 1975

Hedley, O., *Royal Palaces*, Murray, 1975

Hibbert, C., *George IV, Regent and King*, Longmans, 1972

Hillary, R., *The Last Enemy*, Macmillan, 1942

Jenkins, S., *Landlords to London: The Story of a Capital and its Growth*, Constable, 1973

Jesse, J. H., *Memoirs of the Court of England from the Revolution in 1688 to the Death of George II*, Bentley, 1843

Jesse, J. H., *Memorials of London*, 1847

Jesse, J. H., *Memoirs of the Court of England during the Reign of the Stuarts*, 1855

Kingsford, E. L. (ed.), *A Survey of London by John Stow*, Oxford, 1908

Larwood, J., *The Story of the London Parks*, 1881

Little, B., *English Historical Architecture*, 1957

Lloyd, A., *The Wickedest Age*, David and Charles, 1972

Mackay, C., *Through the Long Day*, 1887

Marples, M., *Poor Fred and the Butcher*, Joseph, 1972

Maxwell,Sir H. (ed.), *Thomas Creevey Papers*, Murray, 1903

Milne, Gustav, *The Great Fire of London*, Historical Publications Ltd., 1986

Newton, D., *London West of the Bars*, Hale, 1951

Russel-Barker, G. F. & Le Marchant, Sir D. (eds.), *Walpole's Memoirs of the Reign of George III*, Bodley Head, 1910

Sala, G. A., *Twice Round the Clock*, Houlston Wright, 1859

Scott, J. M., *A Book of Pall Mall*, Heinemann, 1965

Sedgewick, R. (ed.), *Lord Hervey's Memoirs of the Reign of George II*, Eyre & Spottiswoode, 1931

Shepherd, J. E., *Memorials of St. James's Palace*, 1894

Stevens, F. L., *Under London*, Dent, 1939

Strachey, L. & Fulford, R. (eds.), *The Greville Memoirs*, Macmillan, 1938

Strickland, A., *Lives of the Queens of England*, Colburn, 1840

Thomson, A. T. (ed.), *Memoirs of Sarah, Duchess of Marlborough*, H. Colburn, 1839

Timbs, J., *Romance of London*, R. Bentley, 1865

Timbs, J., *Curiosities of London*, 1867

Timbs, J., *London and Westminster*, 1868

Toynbee, P. (ed.), *Letters of Horace Walpole*, 1903

Trevelyan, Sir G., *Charles James Fox*, 1880

Turner, E. S., *The Court of St. James*, 1959

Underwood, P., *Haunted London*, Harrap, 1973

Wellard, J., *By the Waters of Babylon*, Hutchinson, 1972

Wheatley, H. B., *Round About Piccadilly and Pall Mall*, Smith Elder & Co., 1870

Wheatley, H. D. (ed.), *Samuel Pepys's Diary, 1660-1669*, 1893

Williams, H. (ed.), *Jonathan Swift's Journal to Stella, 1713*, 1948

Woodham-Smith, C., *Queen Victoria*, Hamish Hamilton, 1972

Index

130